Russell McCarley

the architecture of glass: shaping light

Author

Francisco Asensio Cerver

Editorial manager

Paco Asensio

Project coordinator

Anna Puyuelo Abad (Architect)

Graphic Design

Mireia Casanovas Soley

Layout

Jaume Martínez Coscojuela

Text

Nadia Casabella, Maurici Pla, Moisés Puente, Anna Puyuelo Abad, Itziar Sen.

Translation

David Buss, Elaine Fradley, Mark Lodge

Copyediting

Michael Webb

Proofreading

Amber Ockrassa

Photographers

Christian Richters (Shopping Center in Emmen, Faculty of Economics, Secondary Schol in Utrecht, Renovation and Enlargement of the Twenthe National Museum); Michael Denancé (Jean-Baptiste Berlier Hôtel Industrielle); Nacása & Parthers Inc., Shinkenchiku, Shinichi Ogawa, Hiroyuki Hirai (Glass House); Mitsumasa Fujitsuka (Museum of Fruit); Herman H. van Doorn (Law Faculty) Nacása & Parthers Inc., Timothy Hursley (International Forum); Nacása & Parthers Inc. (Pachinko Parlor II and III); Busam/Richter Architekturphoto (New exhibition center); Georges Fessy, Hervé Abbadie (Le Palais des Beaux-Arts de Lille); Philippe Ruault (Galeries Lafayette); Margherita Spiluttini (Warehouse for Ricola); Michael Reisch (Neanderthal Museum); Hisao Suzuki (Electrical Grid Building); Kim Zwarts (Pathé Multiplex Cinema); Tomio Ohashi (Auditorium Nagaoka).

First published in 1997 by Arco for

Hearts Books International

1350 Avenue of the Americas

New York, NY 10019

Distributed in the U.S. and Canada by

Watson-Guptill Publications

1515 Broadway

New York, NY 10036

Distributed throughout the rest of the world by

Hearts Books International

1350 Avenue of the Americas

New York, NY 10019

1997 © Francisco Asensio Cerver

ISBN: 0-688-15712-2

Printed in Spain

The Architecture of Glass: Shaping Light

Glass, the fusion of silicon oxide, alkalies
and stabilisers, has, since its discovery in
Egypt around 1500 B.C., exercised a
powerful and seductive fascination based
on its most singular characteristic - its
transparency. For centuries its use was
limited to precious objects due to the high
cost involved in the production techniques
known at the time. It was not until the
Middle Ages that glass began to be
used in architecture. This was a revolutionary
advance that allowed interior spaces to be
isolated from the inclemencies of the
weather, while allowing light to enter
and the exterior to be seen. Light and vision
were absolute, and the translucent marble
and alabaster used in religious
buildings was replaced by this noble
new material. The use of glass in architecture
is linked indissolubly with the advances
made in structural calculations and in
technology. Our Gothic cathederals are the

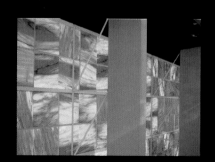

primary example, with their panelled windows progressively occupying more space and reducing the section of the structural elements to the indispensable minimum. It was not until the middle of the nineteenth century when glass again began to have importance as a structural element. The great iron and glass structure of the Crystal Palace, constructed in London for the World Fair of 1851, is the culminating example of this new trend. Since then, the rise of the use of glass as a structural material has been unstoppable. Technological progress, the motor of this renewed use of glass, has once again aimed to include the maximum of glass with the minimum of other structural elements. One example is the curtain wall, a façade made completely of glass, which we see every day. These smooth panels, with a high reflective capacity, remain indifferent to their surroundings and demonstrate how under-used glass is as an element capable of manipulating and modulating light in the interior of buildings.

The massive rise in the use of glass has, unfortunately, not been accompanied by a parallel experimentation in the expressive possibilities that the material undoubtedly possesses. The designs chosen for inclusion in this book are, in our opinion, those which exploit to their full potential some of the most representative characteristics of the material; its transparency; its capacity to create reflections and transform these into the essence of a design, and lastly its translucency, a characteristic shared by materials such as marble and polycarbonate. All the designs included here pose questions as to the real capacity of glass for building with light.

The architecture of glass: shaping light

Shopping Center in Emmen

Ben van Berkel

The new Vroom and Dreesmann shopping center is the result of a total overhaul of an older center built in the 1960s. Van Berkel's plan adds an apartment block, completely reorganizes the layout, and perhaps most importantly, eliminates the old façade, substituting instead a new skin that envelopes the complex and serves as the key to its new identity.

Given that the project calls for the entire building to be reorganized, the plan intelligently reflects the impossibility of achieving a strict planimetric order and does not try to make this the driving force of the design. Instead, the small, continuous irregularities which are normally found in this type of project, the positioning of the stairways, the definitions of the limits of the

Location:

Emmen, The Netherlands.

Date: *1994-1996.*

Client: *Multi Vastgoed bv,*

Gouda.

Builder: *IHN Noord bv,*

Groningen.

Project coordinator:

René Bouman,

Harrie Pappot.

Project manager:

Wilbert Swinkels.

Glass: *HuMa-glas bv.*

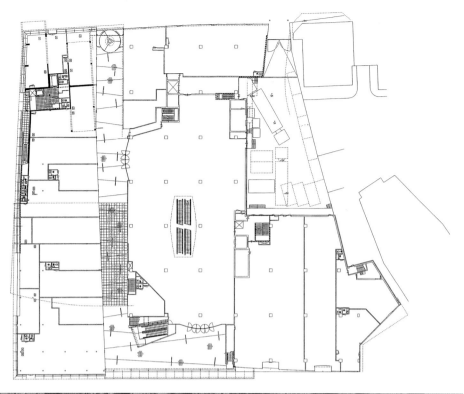

Ground floor.
Below.
*The glass facing is
transparent in some places.*

shops, the continuities between partitions are accepted without prejudices. Van Berkel accepts the characteristic small accidents of the old building, with its repeated alterations of a non-existent geometric order, and works on them one-by-one.

The central part of the complex is occupied by a large hall giving access to the shops placed around the perimeter. Between the hall and the shops there is a corridor that acts as a kind of irrigation channel for all movements. Thus, although lacking geometric order, the building has a conceptual outline which clarifies the whole layout on a general level.

In its volume, the complex is characterized by the bringing together of a series of elements which, taken as a whole, form a system. The ground floor base gives access to some of the shops which can also be reached from the street. The volume of the first floor is converted by Van Berkel into a large, flattened expanse of glass which becomes the main element of the system and unifies it. Above this, a five-floor block with a relatively small surface-houses the apartments in one corner of the complex. A three-floor block whose

Partial view of the west façade. In the foreground, the high apartment block under which the glass facing develops.

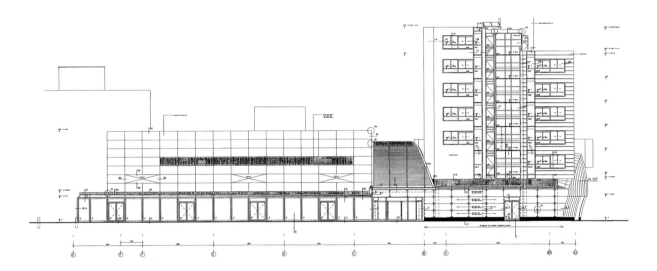

North elevation.

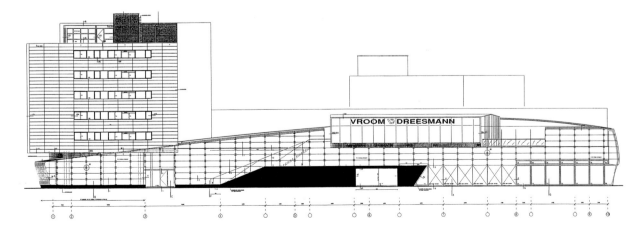

West elevation.

The continuous facing is interrupted by the presence of one of the superior volumes.

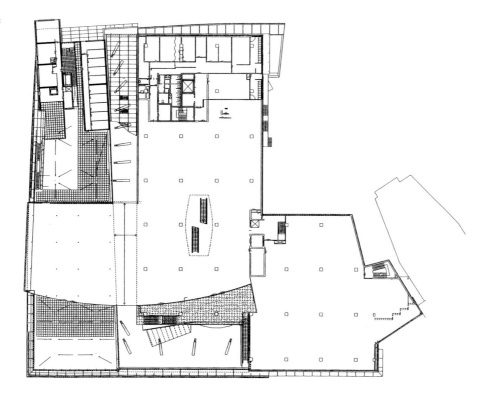

First floor.

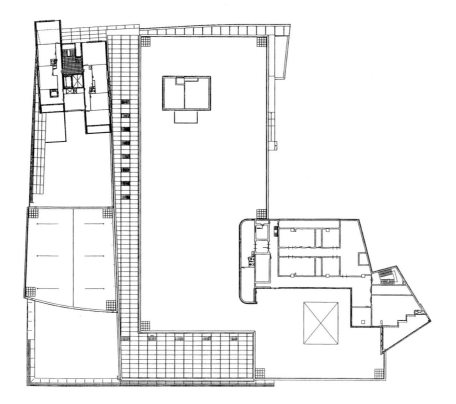

Second floor.

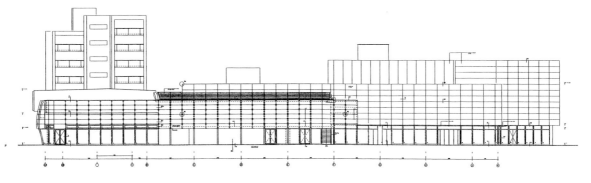

South elevation.

13

Detail of the perimetral glass skin, with its continuous tapering section.

Partial view of the cubic volume, showing different aspects of the translucent glass.

rigorously cubic nature receives special attention, as well as various other intermediate forms which emerge from the great expanse of glass. These are accorded relative importance in relation to the whole, but always without seeking protagonism.

The glass construction is, in reality, not the great mass it appears, but solely a treated façade with an ordered function. A glass screen, without frames, whose section is tapered to produce an aerodynamic shape, is supported by feet of steel arranged in the same form. The construction occupies the façade to a thickness of more than a meter, giving it considerable depth, and even allowing at one point the incorporation of a longitudinal stairway. This cross-sectional pattern is constant throughout the façade, but suffers alter-

ations due to the topographical accidents which it encounters.

At some points, the glass is prolonged to cover other elements, thereby demonstrating its emptiness and the purity and transparency of the glass itself. Alternatively, its crowning line may vary according to the volumes which are encountered, or there appears within it a mysterious protecting balustrade. At times it juts out several metres from the construction it encloses, forming an unusual vertical projection. There is nothing arbitrary about these gestures. Each is a variation on the same theme, motivated by the accidents that this constant curved section meets on its path.

The same system of variations is encountered in the longitudinal course of

Corner between the south and west façades.

General view of the south façade, with the volume of translucent glass in the foreground.

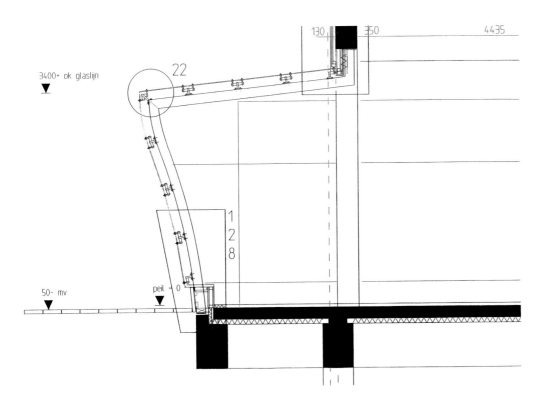

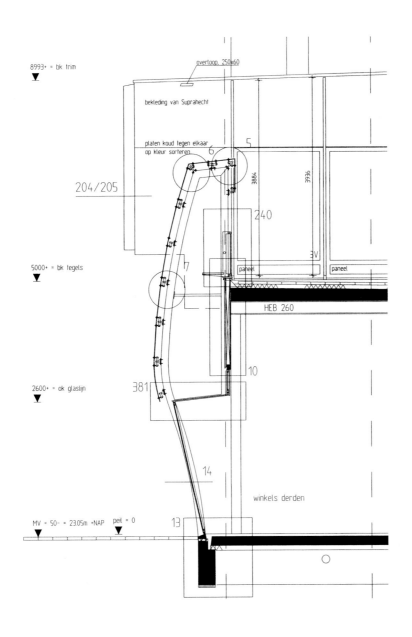

Section of the perimetral glass facing. Detail.

Bellow.
Detail of the perimetral glass facing. Cross section.

the ground floor. The glass may reach down to the ground, following the direction of the supports, or the shop entrances may appear under the glass frieze, or the glass may even be retracted, leaving the supports exposed. In all these cases, however, the cross-section of the glass and its accompanying studs maintain their essential formal characteristics.

This system of longitudinal variations means that the glass can be seen in two ways. Although it is always the same and is always erected in the same way, its trajectory offers very different reflections, transparencies, distorted effects, artificial luminosities, and dark opacities.

Some of the other volumes of the complex are enclosed by other types of glass, such as the very different plaques of translucent glass which finish the prismatic three-story block. This only highlights the way in which Van Berkel resolves the volumetric unity of the shopping center by means of a reduced range of variations on the theme of glass, which, in their reciprocal combinations and their relation with the surroundings demonstrate a variety of effects.

General view of the south façade,
showing where the glass skin
meets the cubic volume.

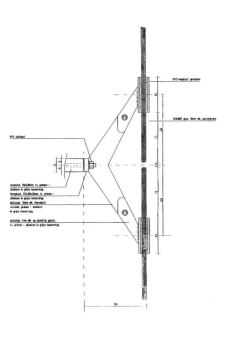

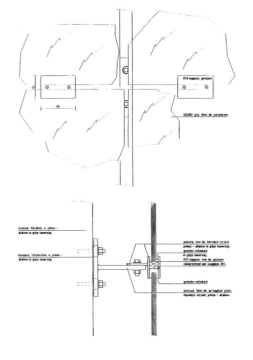

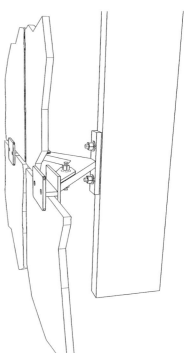

Detail of the anchoring of the glass elements to the metal structure. Horizontal section.

Frontal elevation and vertical section.

Conical perspective.

Previous page.

Partial view of the west façade.

Right.

Partial view of the west façade.

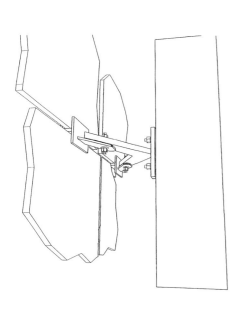

Faculty of Economics

Mecanoo

The new building for the Faculty of Economics of Utrecht Polytechnic is located in a part of the de Uithof campus which has come to be known as the "kasbah." Like the cities of Magreb, the area´s urban characteristics are compactness, the low height of the buildings and a marked introspection based on the use of interior patios. The more than 23,500 square meters of the new center are built around three patios and occupy only three floors.

From the beginning, the idea was to create a building that not only met the requirements of the educational program, but also gave students the opportunity to enjoy the building more fully. The provision of a large number of undefined spaces where students can talk, eat, and drink shows an understanding that these activities form just as much a part of student life as does studying.

Access is from the north side, where the areas of communal services meeting rooms, the multimedia library and the restaurant/café are wrapped by a smooth skin of glass. From here, a comb-like system of wings opens out, housing the Faculty´s departments and administration on their

Location:
Utrecht, The Netherlands.
Date of plan: *1991-1992.*
Construction date:
September, 1993 to May, 1995.
Client: *Foundation Financing Exploitation Accomodation Uithof, Utrecht.*
Building: *Hollandse Beton Maatschappij bv. Utrecht.*
Associates artits:
Gera van der Leun,
Henk Metselaar, Linda Verkaaik.
Size of construction:
23,500 square meters.

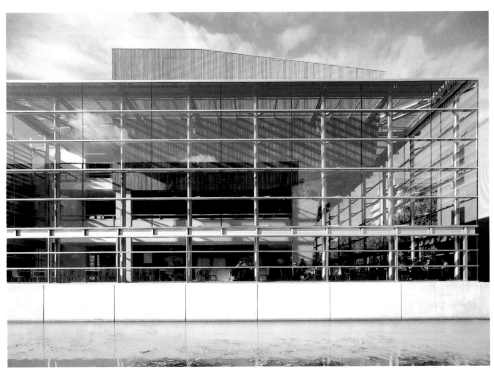

Aerial view of the Faculty
of Economics, sited on
the de Uithof Campus of
Utrecht Polytechnic.

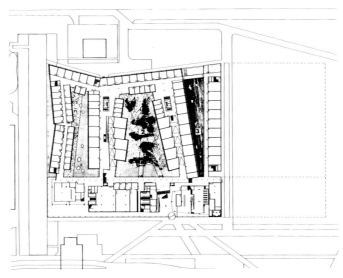

Situation plan of
the campus.

1. Zen Patio.
2. Forest Patio.
3. Water Patio.

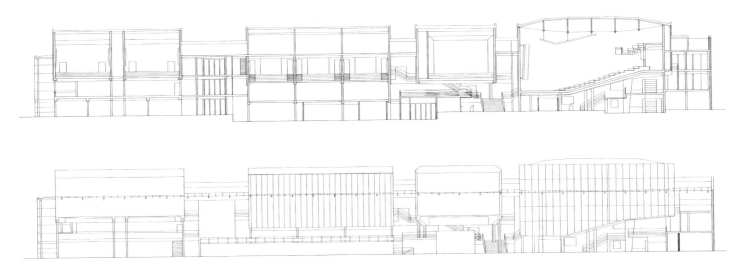

Longitudinal sections of the glass
prism which contains the rooms.

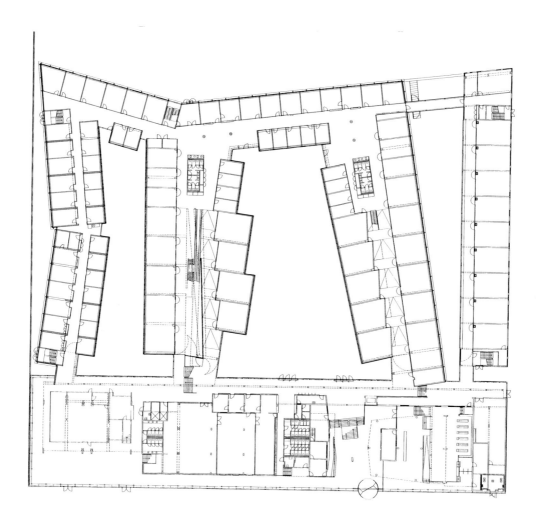

Ground floor.

Interior of one of the rooms.

*View of the structure
of the glass skin.*

*The richly varied spaces
between the rooms facilitate
different activities and uses.*

perimeter, while the classrooms are grouped around the main patio in the central wings.

The north wing is undoubtedly one of the highlights of the design. The four closed boxes which house the various rooms are grouped under a glass roof. The four volumes can be seen through the roof, mixed with reflections of the city and the nearby canal. Each is finished with a different material and the interstices between them are clearly marked by the forthright nature of their design. The large sheet of glass forming the façade has its own metallic structure, which is indepen-

dent of that supporting the four interior volumes, thus accentuating even more the difference between the enveloping skin and what is contained within. The spaces which appear between the façade, the floor of varying height and the volumes of the enclosed rooms, form a series of corners and niches which can house a variety of activities.

The central hall gives access on all three floors to the corridors which lead to the classrooms, the various departments and the administration areas. The two central wings unfold in a succession of impressive ramps, some hanging from roof ties, which

cross the narrow corridors and give access to the classrooms. The ramps are complemented by stairs lit by overhead lighting, which unite the different levels.

The markedly different characters of the patios in the center of the building imbue it with a variety of environments. The Zen patio, which takes its inspiration from notions of Japanese gardens, is covered by large rocks and two different types of gravel, while two delicate trees complete the calm oriental nature of the space. At the other end of the complex, the water patio has views of the surrounding canals and green fields. The reflections, the

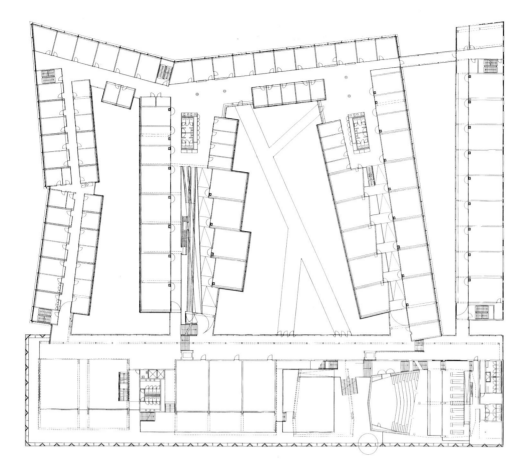

First floor.

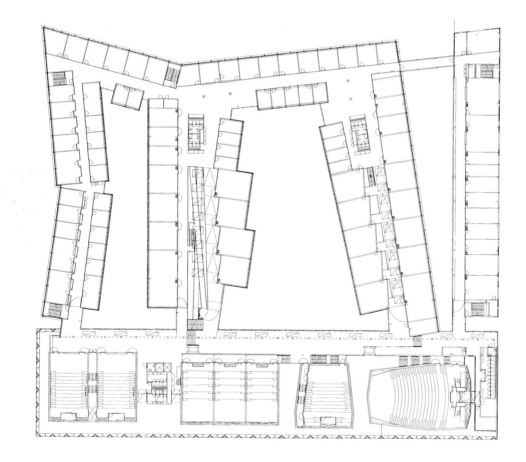

Second floor.

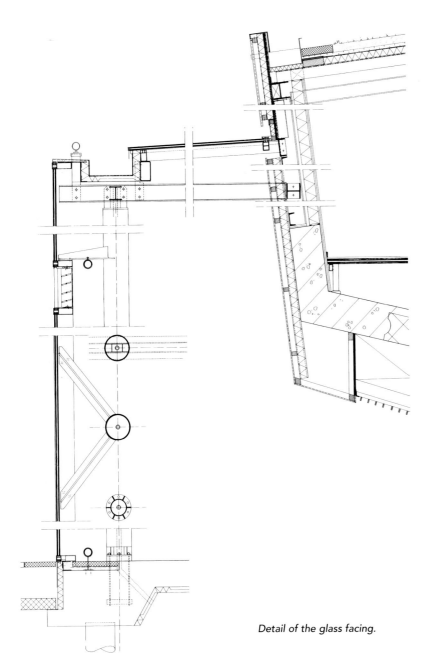

Detail of the glass facing.

changing light, and the passing of the seasons ensure that its appearance is constantly in flux. The larger central patio has the most activity and movement. Its theme is the forest, and it is covered by bamboo of different varieties, heights, and colors. Crossed by walkways which connect the recreation areas grouped around it, the patio is a dynamic space, erasing the boundaries between the interior and exterior of the building.

The façades of the patios are also of different materials. Cedarwood lattices and panels of okumen surround the Zen patio. Glass and metalwork enclose the central one, while the water patio is faced with the same type of aluminum sheeting used for the perimeter of the building.

View of the north access façade.

Exterior view over the canal.

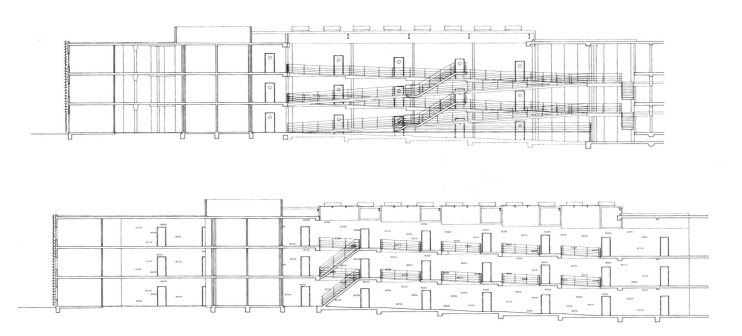

Sections of the ramped corridors.

A glass passageway opens up the water patio to the surrounding countryside.

Forest patio. Exterior walkways penetrate the bamboo, linking the different recreational spaces around the patio on the first floor.

The Zen Patio, with Japanese inspirations, provides a calm, contemplative space. The façades combine latticework and okumen panels.

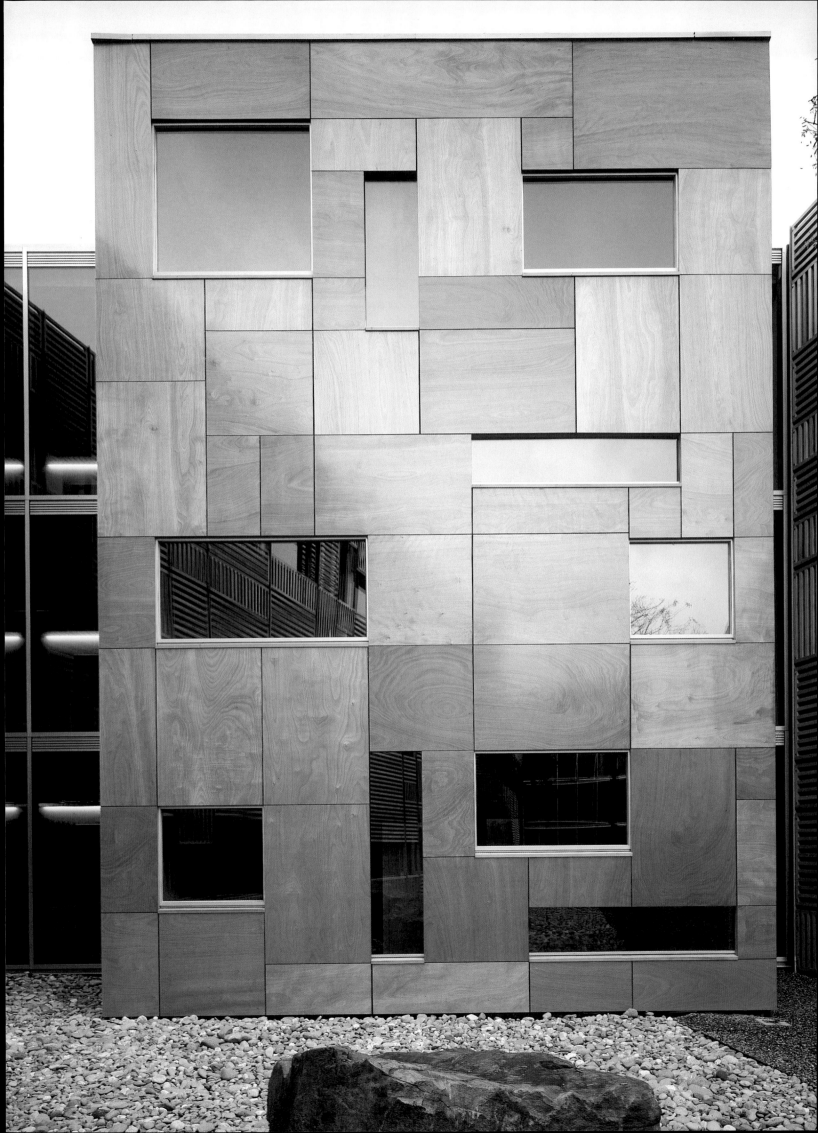

Jean-Baptiste Berlier
Hôtel Industrielle

Dominique Perrault

In 1986, the Paris City Council and the Société Anonyme de Gestion Immobilière organized a competition to come up with solutions for a new type of building: an industrial hotel. Rather than an office block or industrial building, this simply called for an intelligent space to house a variety of activities. The construction of a new type of building was not the only challenge: the site chosen required careful development in a complex area between the Paris ring roads and the rail line leading out of the Gare d'Austerlitz.

The building rises up like a crystal prism. It seems completely indifferent to its set-ting in an area of future development in east Paris, district 13 well communicated with city approach roads amidst cement silos and heliports. Faced with the apparent disorder of its surroundings, the clarity of Perrault's proposal gives the area an entirely new identity.

The building totals 17,000 square meters for industrial activities of various scopes. Each activity is simply provided with open-plan space in the building, connected to installation services. The only conditions are the physical limits of the block and the communication nuclei. Each firm establish-ing business here will pay for only as many

Location:

26-34 Rue Bruneseau,

75013 París, France.

Project: *1986-1988.*

Construction:

1988-1990.

Client: *Société Anonyme de Gestion Immobilière.*

Program:

Industrial premises with restaurants and parking.

Built surface area:

21,000 square meters.

Space inside, for rent.

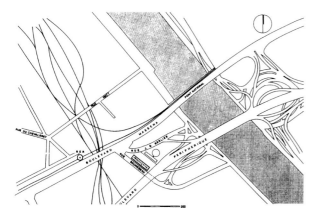

Ground plan of location.

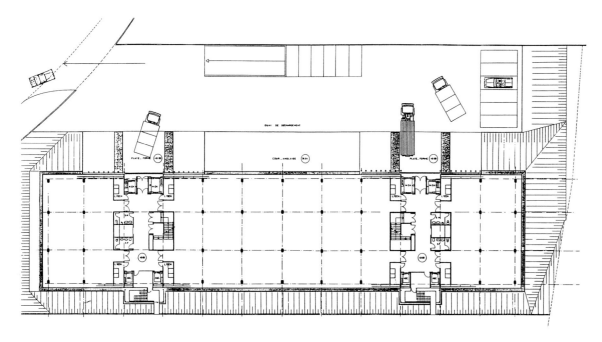

First floor.

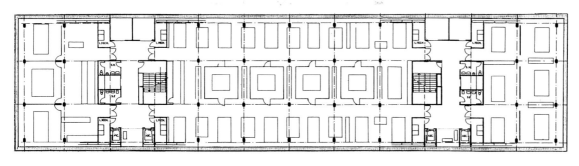

Model floor plan with possible occupation.

square meters as it requires: some industries will expand and others will disappear. No form or explicit architectural style is imposed on them; it is the transparency of the block which reveals the changing lives of its occupants.

With a view to maintaining this image of a glazed prism, the structural elements and installations are housed inside, while the glass-dividing elements display a minimum of frame. The electrical and air-conditioning installations are housed visibly between the structure and façade; together with horizontal metal-slat brise-soleil screens, this effect protects the façade, endowing it with a degree of depth. Metal struts starting on the inside support the façade installations, freeing the taut glass curtain from any obstacles which might interfere with a clear view of the building as a prismatic volume. From the outside, the tubes and housing of the brise-soleil screens are visible through the glass, creating a modulation of the façade different from the glass frames. Rather than providing a display, this inner façade is there to create a rhythm in the space between the floors.

The building is completely air-conditioned, and none of the glass panels can be opened, though some can be broken to provide escape in the event of fire. The double anti-reflective glass panels in the façade are treated to reduce sunlight by 52% and provide soundproofing of 35 dB.

The glass façade gives a clear
view of activity inside.

Occupied interior.

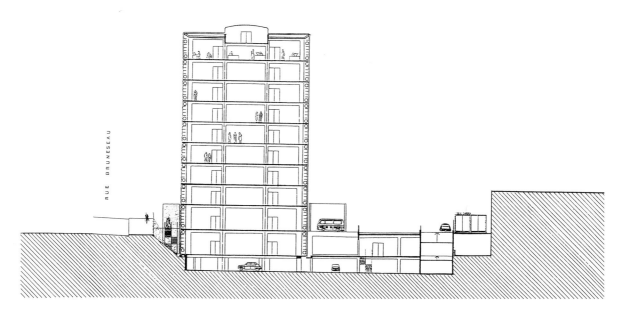

Cross-section.

The empty building displays its layout very clearly.

Night view. The changing occupants and activities change the building's appearance.

Detail of the façade.

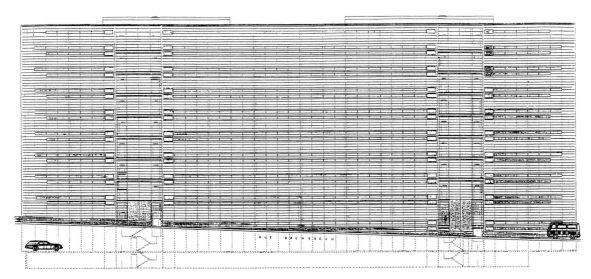

Northwest elevation.

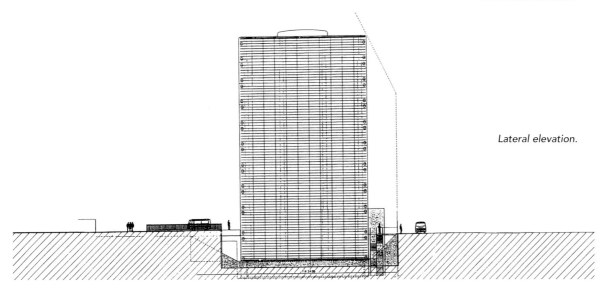

Lateral elevation.

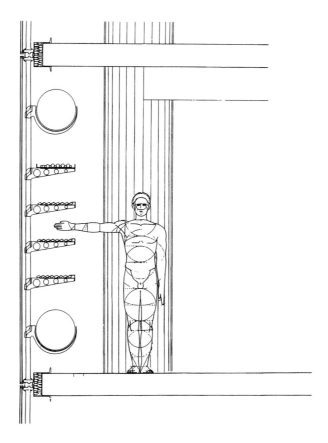

Detail of the façade with installations.

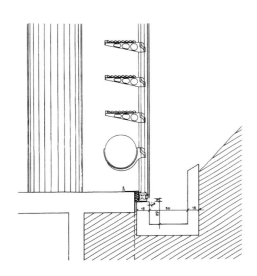

*Detail of the façade where
it meets the ground.*

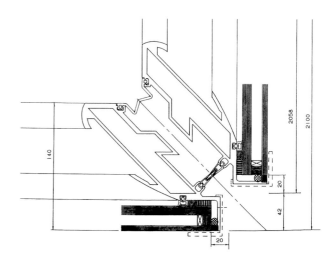

*Detail showing how the
frames adapt to corners.*

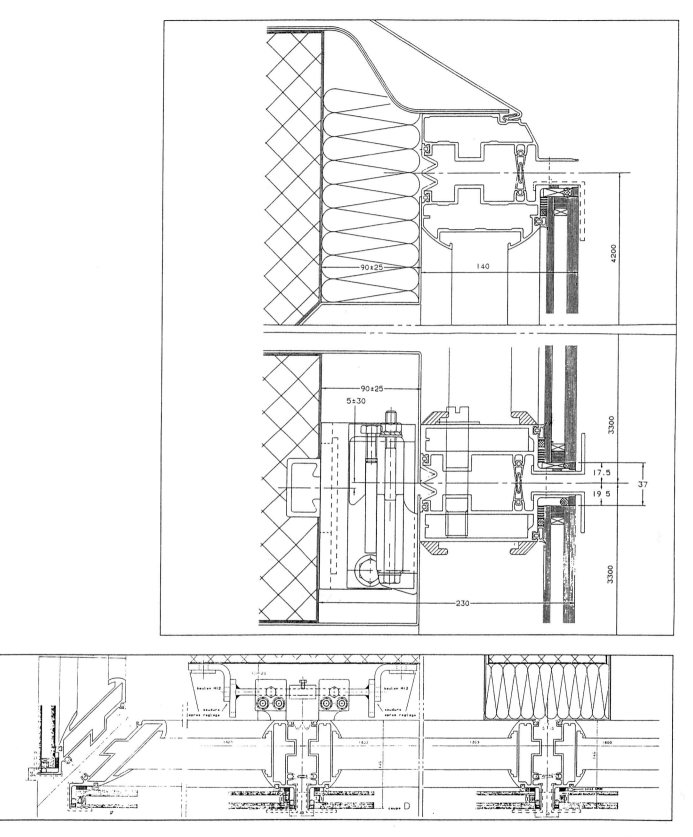

Details of the frame
employed in the façade.

Glass House

Shinichi Ogawa

This plot of land on the outskirts of Hiroshima, on the estuary of the river Hachiman, is the site for a three-story, glass-walled parallelepiped. The first and second floors are the living quarters of the owner, who is an architect, and the third floor is the owner's office.

The building is an autonomous element with its own laws, set apart from its surroundings, with which it makes no attempt to establish a formal relationship. Japanese suburbia is characterized by its division into highly populated plots of land, where each owner sets up independently of neighbors. The result is a thick carpet of single-family houses which do not communicate architecturally with adjacent buildings. The expression of their volume does not emerge from a dialogue with place; it is self-imposed, creating its own limits.

This is also the case of Shinichi Ogawa's house. Perhaps paradoxically, in view of the fact that it is made of glass, a material which for its very nature would seem to

Location: *Nishi Ward, Hiroshima, Japan.*
Completion date: *November, 1995.*
Builder: *Bell Corporation.*
Structural: *Uesugi Structural Engineers.*

The stairways joining all the floors; its various wall structures show up against the masonry side wall.

promote direct relations with its setting. However, this office/home prefers a relationship with the sky, with light, and to the urban landscape around it. This premise helps us understand the morphology of the first floor.

A new ground level has been constructed, thereby extending the available surface with the construction of two completely solid concrete walls with no openings. They stand 1.5 and 4.5 meters away from the north and south façades which mark out two patios, accessible from inside the house. It is these walls which guarantee the privacy of the living room, kitchen, and bathroom, all with their doors facing north. Two stairways, one at either end of the house, lead to the upper floors. Entrance to the west stairway is on the street, as it leads to the public sector of the building, with the architect's studio on the top floor. The stairway on the eastern side leads to the second floor of the house with just four bedrooms in a row, all of which can be secluded by mobile panels made of insulating material.

It is on the third and relatively public floor that the glazed parallelepiped emerges in all its transparency, with no nuances interjected by a need for privacy. This floor is 6 meters high twice the height of the lower floors following the original three-dimensional framework that divides the volume into four parts, with one mod-

ule for each of the domestic stories and two modules for the office floor.

In terms of structure, the building is in no way complex; it is resolved on clean, clear lines and relegates technical complexity to the construction details which make the volume air-tight. The structure comprises five parallel gantries running across the volume with a six-meter bay, at a distance of three meters. The pillars are placed at a distance of 30 centimeters from the façades, so that façade and structure function independently.

The frames holding the glass panels, anchored in the floor-to-ceiling structures of each floor, are self-supporting, and tolerate minor distortions. The architect's meticulous attention to the upper limit of the cornice turning it to create a narrow strip in the roof, thereby creating one more glass edge, shows his determination to apply the same formal laws to his treatment of volume.

Night view of the west façade. While in daylight we perceive the uniformity of the parallelepiped, at night it becomes a succession of wall structures and a roof illuminated by artificial light.

View of the southern façade of the patio, facing the floor with the bedrooms and the studio on the top floor.

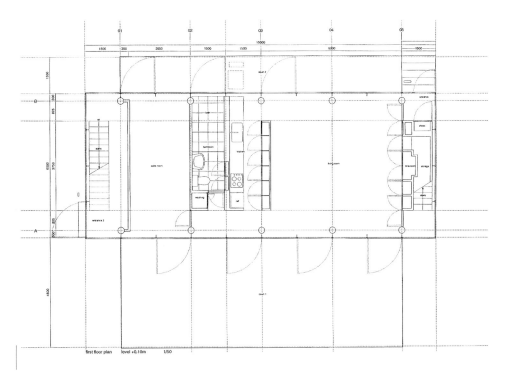

Ground floor of the house. The layout of the rooms follows a strip pattern: living room, kitchen and bathroom, and guest room, with the stairways at either end.

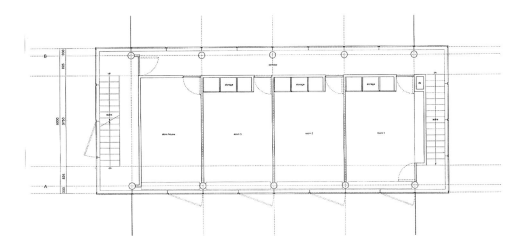

First floor with bedrooms.

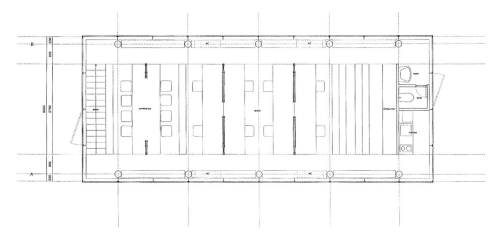

Double-height second story containing the studio. The west stairway leads directly from the street to its meeting room and work area.

Sunset seen from the studio.
The glass façade turns to create
a cornice and extends to meet
the concrete roof.

The house, seen from the east.

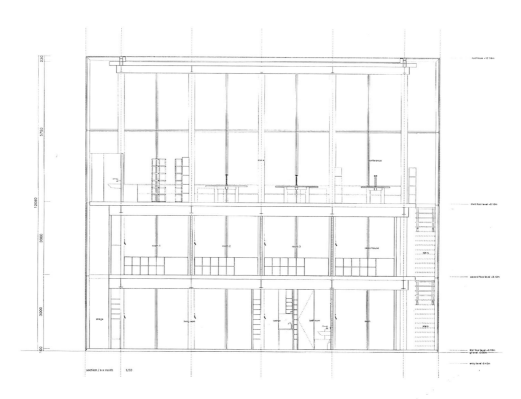

Longitudinal view. Detailed observation of the junction
of the glass skin and the structure of the various floors
gives us a clearer understanding of the project.

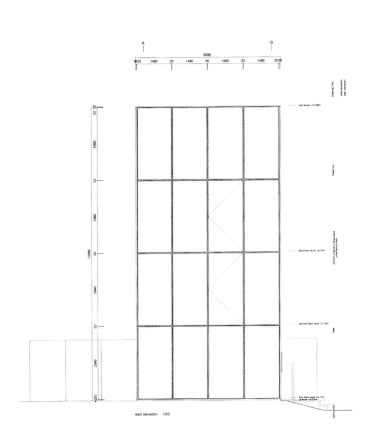

east elevation 1/50

East elevation.

View of the house and its surroundings.

The patio to the south on a fine day.

section / y-y west 1/50

Cross-section

Museum of Fruit

Itsuko Hasegawa

The original idea for building the Museum of Fruit came from the Prefecture of Yamanashi, which is one of the areas of greatest fruit production in all Japan. The site chosen for this unusual museum was a public park, which is surrounded by large vineyards and which enjoys extensive views over the city.

From the first moment, the metaphors of vitality and diversity, almost inherent in the nature of fruit, imbued the spirit of the new project. Historically, fruit has been seen as an aesthetic object, something worthy of veneration, with religious and magical undertones. This inspired a certain poetry in the architecture of the new museum, in an attempt to evoke all the spiritual and social values which these plants represent.

Three relatively small cabin-style buildings of differing shapes and sizes metaphorically represent the life cycle of fruit. The plaza represents the final image of the growth of the seed, with the great trees that are both the result of the process and the generators of a new cycle of life. The square is covered by a flattened glass cupola.

The greenhouse is a kind of encyclopedia of fruit, dedicated to the tropical sun which germinates so many seeds. Covered by an oval-shaped glass cupola, its basement houses the exhibition rooms of the

Location:

Yamanashi City, Japan.

Completion date:

August, 1995.

Client:

Prefecture of Yamanashi.

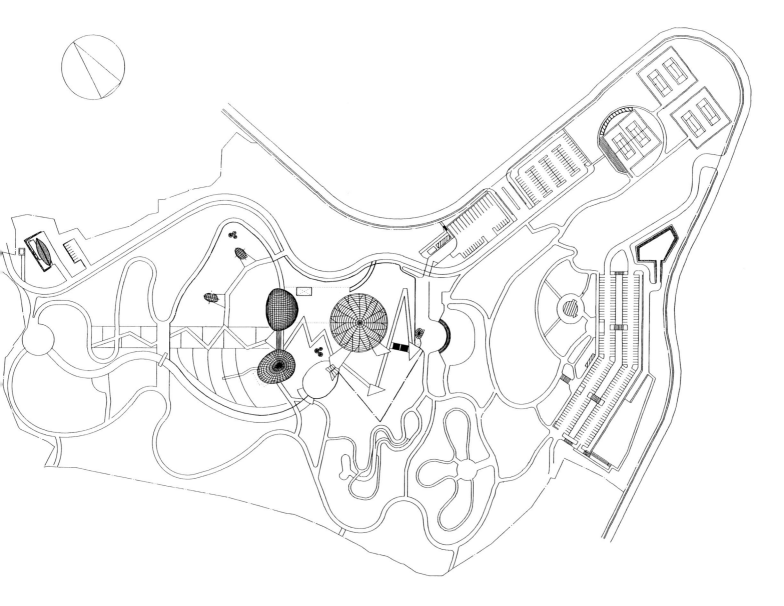

museum itself, which are connected with the plaza subterraneously. A didactic exhibition explains various aspects of fruit cultivation and innovations in the field of genetics.

Another building houses workshops, a library and other educational services, and on the upper floor, a café with spectacular panoramic views over the city. A three-dimensional unfaced mesh gives the feeling of being under a roof.

The complex offers various interpretations to the visitor, who may be fascinated by the world of seeds or by the futuristic park, the botanical garden from the past century, or looking toward a new era. The unusual volumes which comprise the complex seem like seeds borne on the wind, either recently landed or ready to take off; their alighting in one particular place being a mere whim of chance.

Site plan of the complex
with the public park.

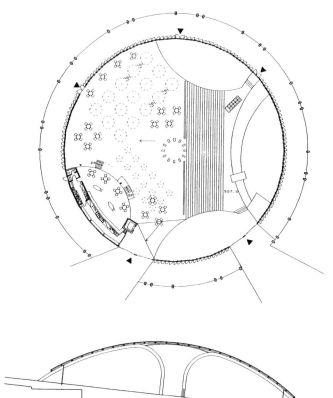

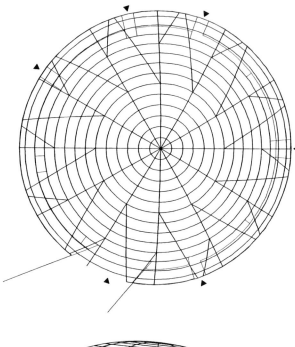

Plaza. Elevation and section.

Exterior view of the greenhouse.

Interior of the greenhouse.

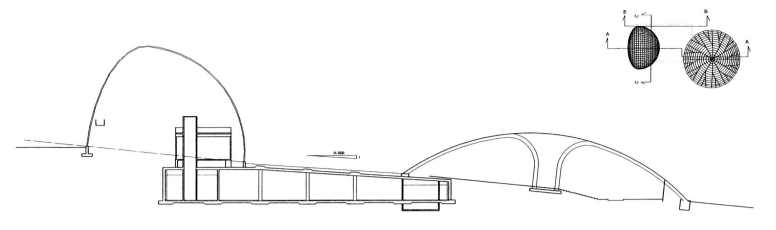

A-A' Longitudinal section of the greenhouse and of Fruit Square.

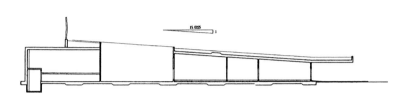

B-B' Longitudinal section of the underground level.

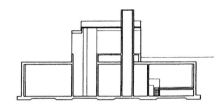

C-C' Cross section of greenhouse.

Floors of the building containing the workshops and café.

Panoramic views from the café.

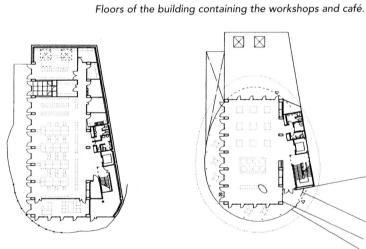

Underground floor.

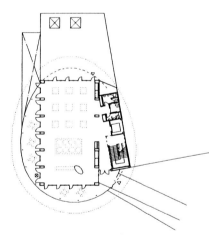

Ground floor.

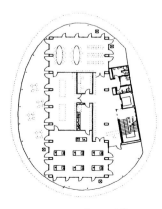

Second floor.

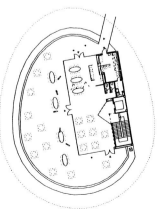

Third floor.

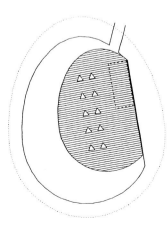

Roof.

Law Faculty, Cambridge

Norman Foster

In 1990, the University of Cambridge announced a limited competition for the construction of a new Law Faculty and Institute of Criminology. The project was to be built in two phases, in a relatively small area bearing in mind how many built square meters it involved. The winning solution by Norman Foster's team outlines two L-shaped buildings; the first phase, the Law Faculty, is now complete.

The site is on the Sidwick campus itself,

beside the famous James Stirling History Faculty. The idea was to minimize the apparent size of the buildings, set amidst lawns and established trees, so as to respect the garden-like atmosphere. The two buildings conclude in a wedge with a strip of garden between them to preserve an old maple tree and a clear view of the History Faculty. This sensitive, conservative attitude to the campus setting contrasts with the dynamism that the building

Location: *University of Cambridge, Great Britain.*
Completion date: *October, 1995.*
Client: *University of Cambridge.*
Structures: *Anthony Hunt Associates.*
Library capacity: *120,000 volumes.*
Total surface area: *9,000 square meters.*

The outside of the northwest corner.

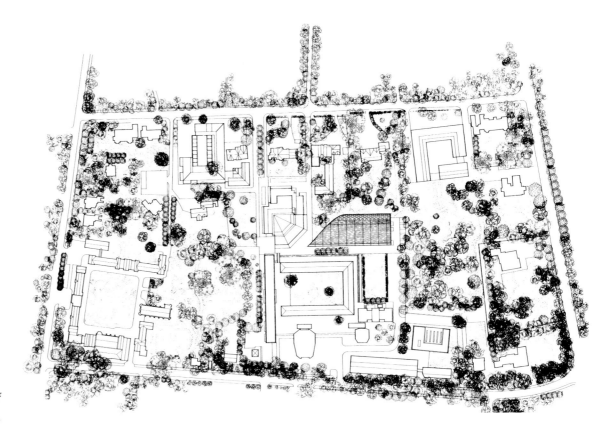

Ground plan of
location on campus.

West façade.

Access to the building. A bite out of the volume at its southwest corner.

South façade.

Night view of the west side of the entrance hall.

acquires by means of simple but forceful operations on its volume, making it the focal point of the campus.

The new faculty holds seminar rooms, meeting rooms, five lecture halls, offices and a major library, covering a total of 9,000 square meters and spread out over six stories. Two of the floors are basements to keep the building in line with the present skyline of the campus. The first floor holds multipurpose classrooms, offices and other staff-related spaces. The basement floors hold three large halls, book storage, and student meeting rooms, and the three remaining floors are set aside for the library.

Entry from the southwest cuts into the angular volume of the wedge and leads into a hall which runs the entire height of the building, providing access to all floors. A large opening lets light into the students meeting room in the basement. A narrow strip for services and administration offices occupies the south-facing façade, while the north façade curves in a glazed surface to overlook the gardens. The library floors are staggered to adapt to the curved façade without ever touching it, allowing the reading rooms to receive unobstructed daylight. The area of visual contact between the various floors means that the large curved façade is

Night view of the north façade.

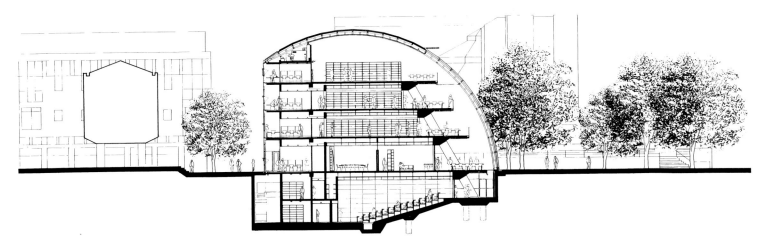

Cross north-south section.

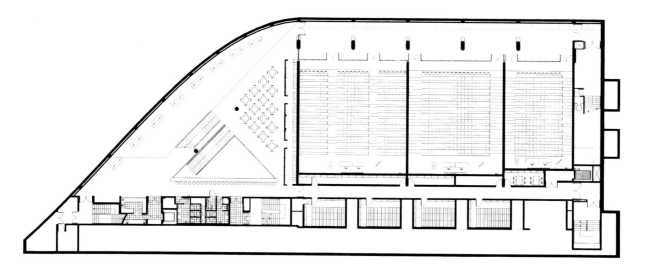

Basement floor.

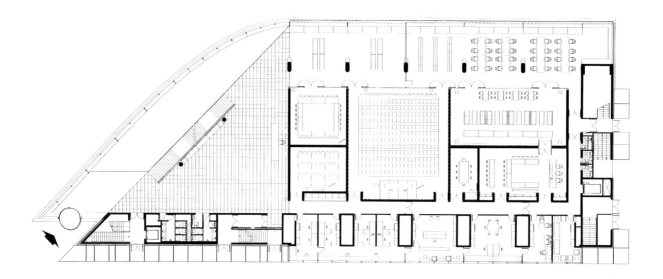

Ground floor.

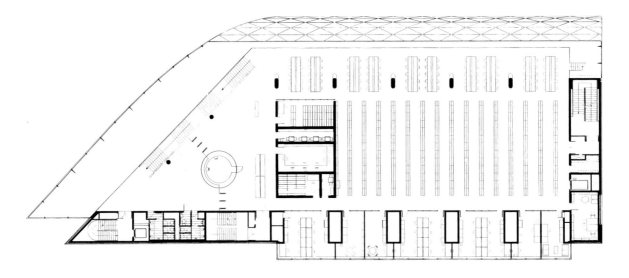

Second floor.

Detail of the entrance corner.

North-facing façade.

West façade.

Detail of the south-facing façade.

On the previous page.
Interior of the entrance hall,
running the entire height
of the building.

The floor to ceiling panels
do not touch the north-
facing façade, leaving space
for vistas over the gardens.

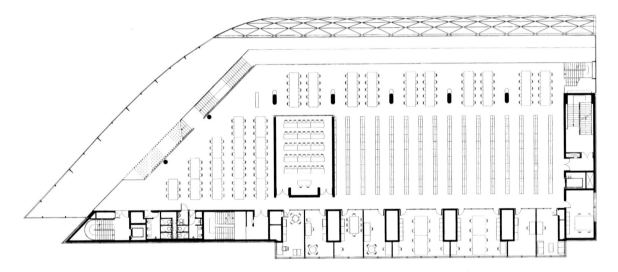

Third floor.

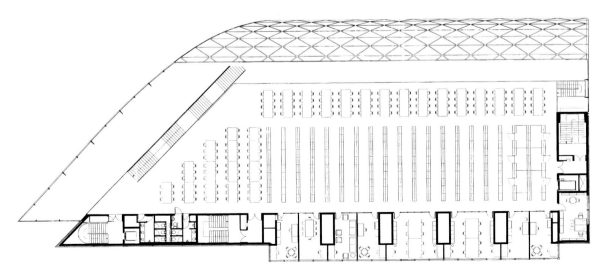

Fourth floor.

*View over the gardens
from the reading rooms.*

always visible, and gives a complete view of the whole building as it follows this line or of the garden beyond.

Seen from the outside, the north-facing façade is made up of glass panels joined by structural silicone. Where the façade joins the roof, the panels are replaced by stainless steel to prevent too much exposure to the sun. The structure of the curved surface is independent of the floor-to-ceiling structures, and is made of a three-dimensional, triangular mesh. The west façade arches in a sinusoidal curve to

resolve the 45-degree cut of the volume's cylindrical form. The south-facing façade uses glass with solar protection and untreated Portland stone.

The points of anchorage of the curved façade are joined to six-bar intersections in the metal structure supporting the façade. These anchors are adjusted in three directions to facilitate the structure's movement and tolerance. The sealed glass panels are supported by industrial aluminum frames which produce the pattern of the façade.

Detail of the points of anchorage of the glass panels to the façade structure.

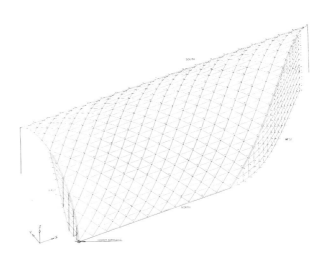

Movement and pattern of the glass panels in the curved surface.

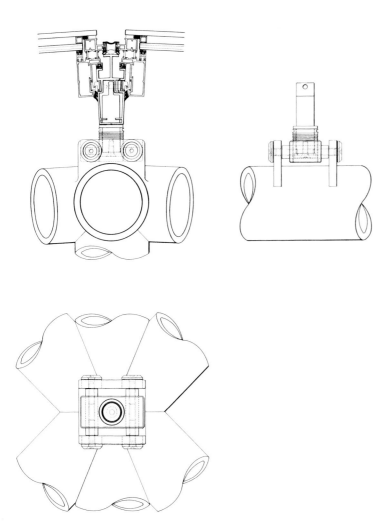

Details of the points of anchorage of the glass panels to the three-dimensional tubular structure supporting the façade.

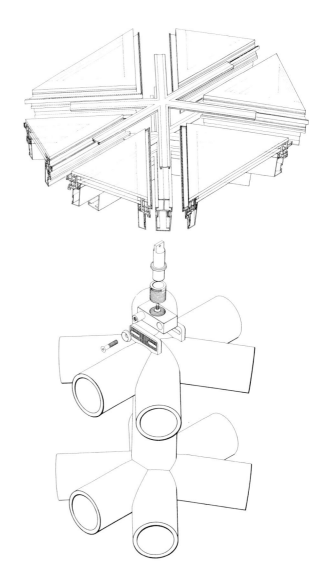

New exhibition center, Leipzig

Von Gerkan, Marg & Partner

This enormous exhibition complex for Leipzig follows a long tradition of trade fairs in this German city. The efforts now being made by a unified Germany to revitalize the former democratic republic make this trade fair precinct one of the major commercial meeting points between Eastern and Western Europe.

This new trade fair site is located on the northern outskirts of the city of Leipzig, and is well communicated with major city approach roads and the airport. As well as the usual trade fair facilities, this project includes places for the organization of complementary congresses and meetings, with a view to bringing attendants, experts and users together.

A limited competition was organized in 1991, with fourteen teams from all over the world being invited to take part. The Hamburg firm GMP, in collaboration with landscape architects Wehberg, Eppinger and Schmidtke, came out winners with their dense urban proposal set in a linear structure organized around a large central foyer.

One of the keys to the development of the complex was keeping the circulation separate on two different levels. A first-

Location: *Messeallee 1, Leipzig, Germany.*
Competition date: *1992.*
Dates of construction: *1993-1996.*
Client: *Leipziger Messegesellschaft.*
Façade consultant: *PBI, Klaus Glass, Büro Wronn.*
Structures: *Ian Ritchie Architects, London.*
Lanndscape architects: *Wehberg, Eppinger, Schmidtke.*

Western entrance to the great foyer.

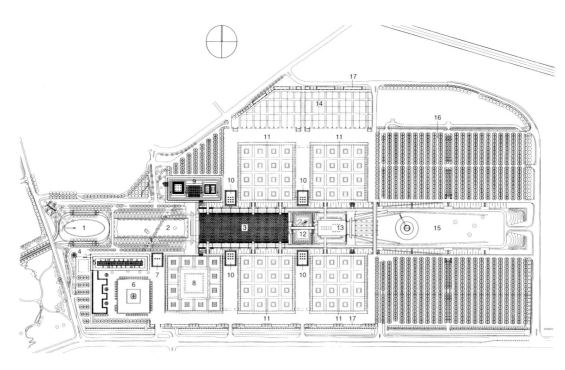

1. Trade fair entrance.

2. Pool.

3. West entrance foyer.

4. Tower.

5. Administration.

6. Crafts center.

7. Forum.

8. Foyer.

9. Congress center.

10. Restaurant.

11. Exhibition spaces.

12. Park.

13. Eastern foyer.

14. Open-air exhibition.

15. Eastern park.

16. Car parking.

17. Service building.

*Ground plan of the
trade fair complex.*

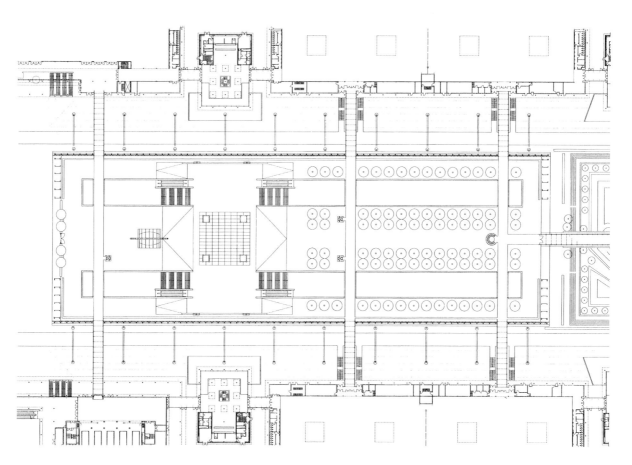

Ground plan of the great foyer.

Western approach to the trade fair.

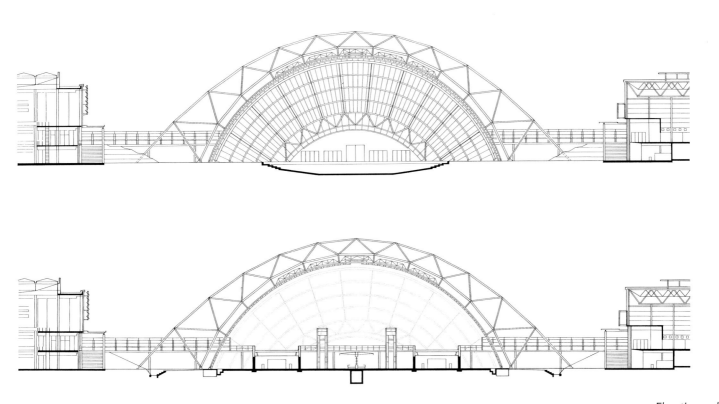

*Elevation and
cross-section of the foyer.*

Previous page.
*Eastern approach to
the domed foyer.*

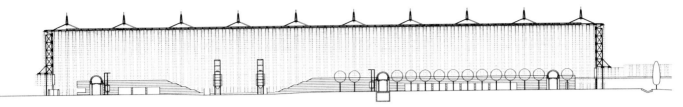

*Longitudinal section
of the foyer.*

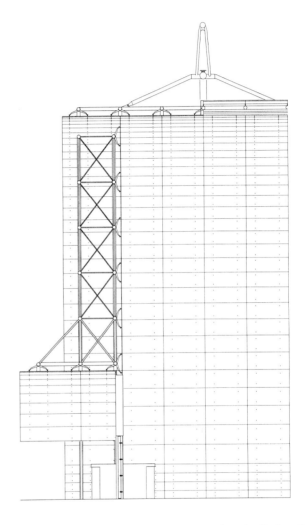

*Longitudinal section of
the western approach.*

Inside the foyer.

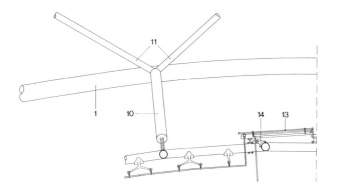

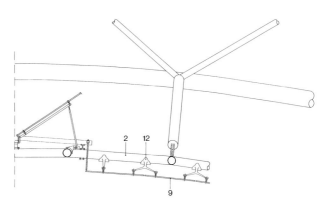

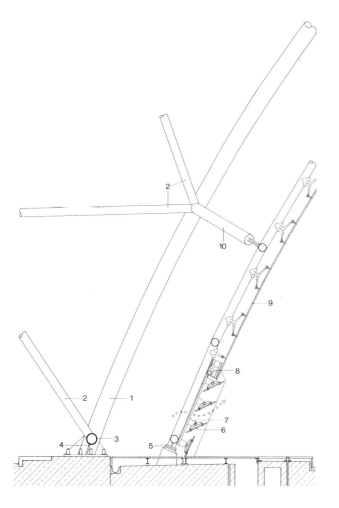

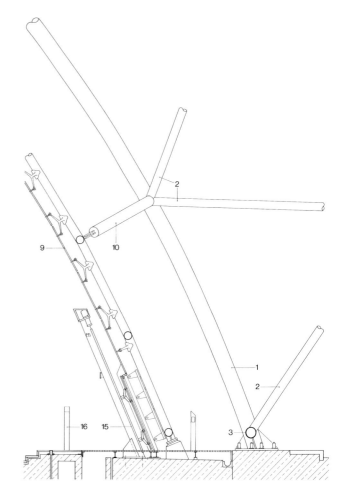

Details of anchorage between
the glass and the bearing structure.

1. 473 x 16 mm steel tube.
2. 244.5 x 8 mm steel tube.
3. 318 x 12.5 mm steel tube.
4. 3 mm plate.
6. 10 mm glass slats.
7. Torsion component.

Construction detail of one of the
emergency doors.

8. The motor which activates the slats.
9. 2 x 10 mm glass.
10. 273 x 8 mm steel tube.
11. 159 x 6.3 mm steel tube.
12. Cast-iron brace with points of
    anchorage for the glass.
14. Motor.
15. Emergency door with
    electromagnetic control.
16. Door-opening mechanism.

floor level provides for the reception, orientation, and distribution of visitors, while the upper floor leads into exhibition and meeting spaces. By increasing the density of construction, distances were kept short, all for the convenience of the user.

The domed space at the center houses various services: tickets, signposts, information points, and access to the upper level. The stone volumes of the stairways lead via communicating galleries and glazed walkways to the other precinct buildings. This great glazed foyer, over 250 meters long and 80 wide, is the largest of its kind ever built. A metal structure on the outside supports a parabolic mesh to which the glass panes are attached and sealed with silicone. At all points, the supports of the glass skin are anchored on the outside, leaving the glass to shine in all its tautness, free of obstacles. On the inside, with a view to making the structure

Detailed view of the structure of the western approach.

Detail of anchorage of the structure's glass.

Office building with the central
foyer in the background.

clearer and more human in scale, the various parts are modulated with a 1.25-meter micromesh to create various hierarchies.

Various measures have been taken to reduce excessive exposure to the sun, with the outer structure shading the exposed surface to reduce sunlight by 15%. Protective strips of a ceramic material have been used to reinforce the dome at its most critical points. Moveable slats are situated around the lower edge to produce natural ventilation.

The administrative building and the congress center, both of which communicate with the central foyer, use state-of-the-art systems for their glazed façades, including a protective outer skin of glass slats.

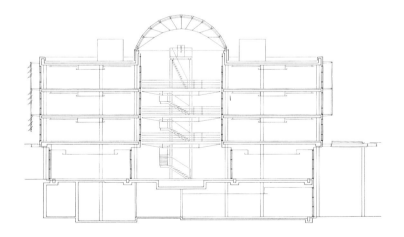

Section of the
office building.

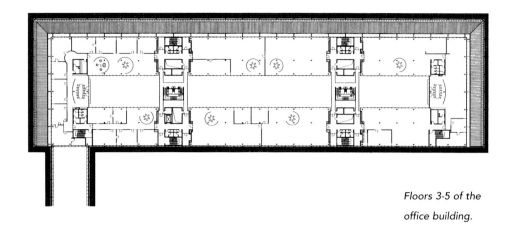

*Floors 3-5 of the
office building.*

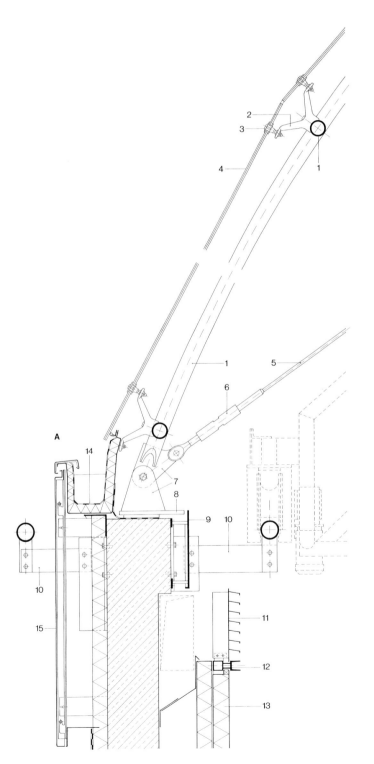

*Construction detail of the dome
of the office building.*

1. 88.9 x 7.1 mm steel tube.

2. Cast-iron brace.

3. Point anchoring the glass.

4. 6 and 8 mm glass.

5. 16 mm cable.

6. Tensor.

7. 15 mm steel plate.

8. 20 mm steel plate.

9. 2 mm sheet cladding.

10. Auxiliary structure.

11. Slat framework.

12. Metal profile.

13. Metal sheet panel for
    interior cladding.

14. Drainage pipe.

15. Metal sheet panel for
    outer cladding.

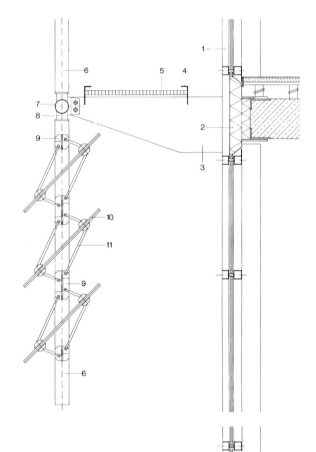

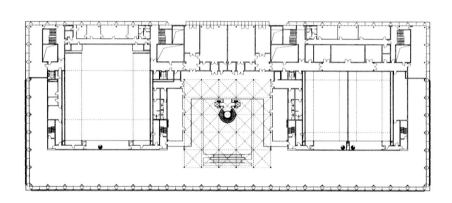

Third floor of the congress center.

Detail of the façade.

1. Aluminum frames.
2. Metal sheet panel for outer cladding.
3. 10 mm support.
4. Steel profile, 50 x 130 x 5 mm.
5. Grille.
6. 108 x 2.9 mm steel tube.
7. 108 x 4.5 mm steel tube.
8. Cast-iron anchorage.
10. 2 x 8 mm glass slats.
11. Tensor to hold the glass slats.
12. Slat framework.
13. IPE 300 steel profile.
14. 100 x 50 steel profile.

Slatted façade of the
congress center.

View of the congress
center across from
the pool.

International Forum, Tokyo

Rafael Viñoly

In 1989, the Tokyo City Council organized an international competition for the construction of a new metropolitan forum in the heart of the city. Out of 395 proposals from all over the world, the New York based team of Uruguayan architect Rafael Viñoly was selected to design this vast complex, an emblem of Japan's blooming economy.

The location, in the downtown district of Marunouchi, a business area close to the commercial district of Ginza, is strategically connected to the subway system as well as to the Tokyo and Yurakucho train stations. The site is near the gardens of the emperor's palace. It was formerly occupied by the city hall and other council buildings designed by Kenzo Tange in 1957. The city hall was demolished in 1991 and those offices were moved to the new skyscrapers in the financial center of Shinjuku.

The project started with the decision to separate the most important parts into different volumes. Four large halls for concerts, exhibitions, and congresses fall in with the urban fabric of their setting, and are spaced out according to size. The large

Location: *3-5-1 Marunouchi, Chiyoda-ku, Tokyo, Japan.*
Competition date: *November 1989.*
Completion date: *June 1997.*
Client: *Tokyo Metropolitan Government.*
Collaborators: *Masao Shiima Architects.*
Structure: *Kunio Watanabe (Structural Design Group).*
Program: *Four halls for theater, concerts, and conferences. The largest hall seats 5000 and the smallest 1500. Also includes exhibition site, offices, shops, restaurants, and parking.*
Total surface area: *145,000 square meters.*

Ground plan of location in the
center of Tokyo.

View of the outdoor public space
between the atrium and halls.

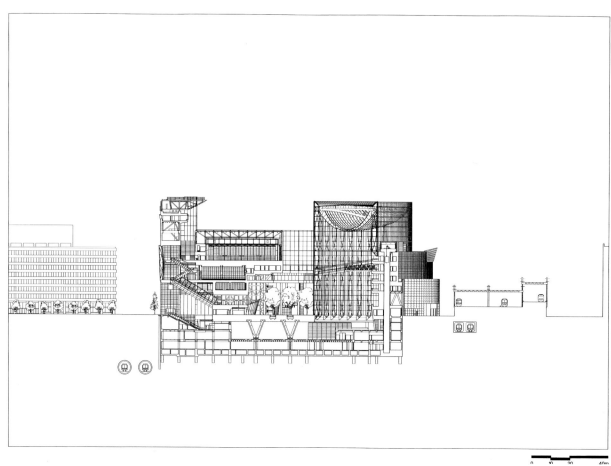

East-west section of the complex.

North-south section through the halls. This major complex is connected to the city's underground transport network.

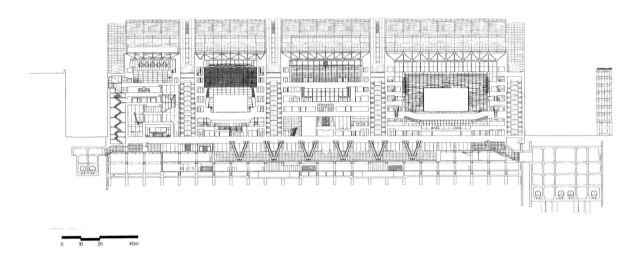

0   10   20   40m

entrance foyer at the opposite end of the site follows the lines of the nearby train tracks to adapt perfectly to the perimeter of the site with its elongated spindle shape. A street wide enough to be a plaza between the entrance foyer and the various halls provides communication not only between the various parts of the project but also with the rest of the city, becoming a valuable public space for Tokyo.

The glazed entrance foyer is the center of attention of the complex. It contains a large block of conference and meeting rooms that open inwards, turning their back on the rail line with an almost completely blind façade. This solid volume is topped by a large glazed atrium, a real tour de force of glass engineering. The solution adopted by Viñoly's team in the original proposal was less audacious in terms of structure, since the roof was supported by twelve large pillars.

The solution was subsequently streamlined in a joint venture with the engineering

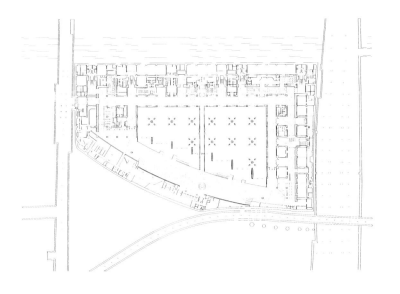

Basement floor: connections
with the transport system.

Ground floor.

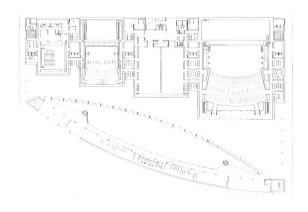

Second floor.

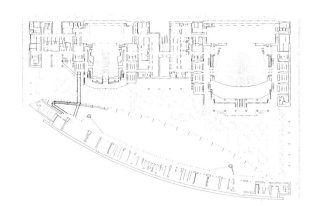

Third floor.

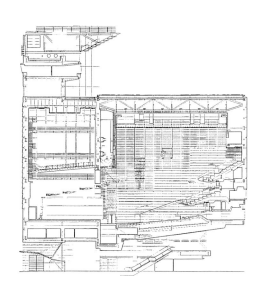

Section of one of the halls, with
seating for 1,500 people.

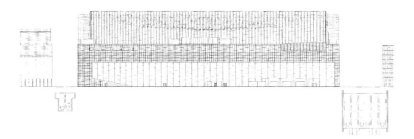

East elevation.

North elevation.

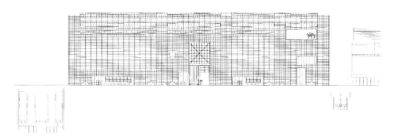

West elevation.

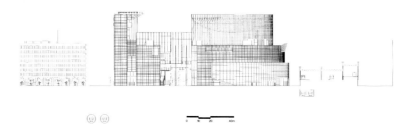

South elevation.

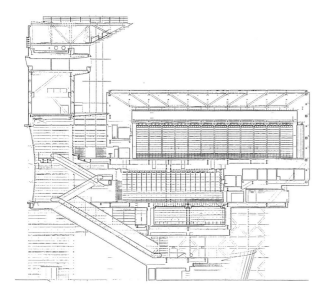

East-west section.

Section through the main hall, a theater with seating for 5,000 people.

team of Kunio Watanabe to produce just two huge pillars, one at each end, supporting the entire structure and covering the 124-meter-long foyer. The columns reach a maximum diameter of four and a half meters in the middle, and are connected to the block of conference halls to provide maximum stability in seismic movements and lateral wind pressure. Seismic considerations have led to a special type of glazed construction which is still unusual in Japan, but that is now technically possible.

The 57-meter-high curtain wall is made up of panels of 16-millimeter-thick plate glass. It is stabilized by a braced auxiliary structure, independent of the roof, which is earthquake resistant. A large circulation ramp was designed in the west façade to make the structure more rigid and absorb lateral wind force on the delicate glass curtain. Pedestrian walkways on levels seven and eight, along with two large struts, ensure that lateral pressure on the façade is passed on to the solid block containing the conference rooms. This spectacular display of technology provides the city with a great public space packed with new spatial experiences at the heart of a Tokyo rushing to meet the coming century.

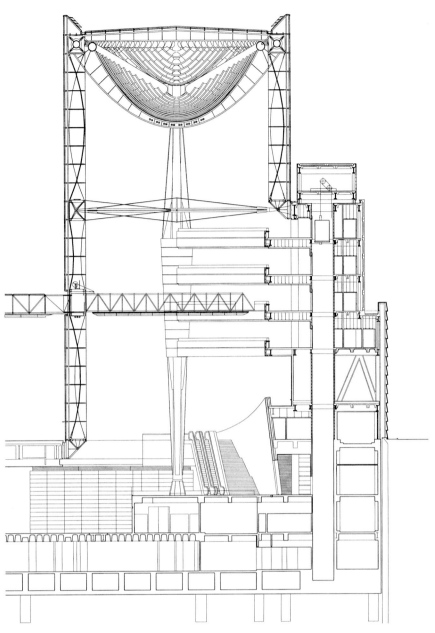

East-west section through the atrium.

Night-time lighting of the atrium.

Inside the atrium. Walkways and struts give this delicate, glass-panel structure greater rigidity.

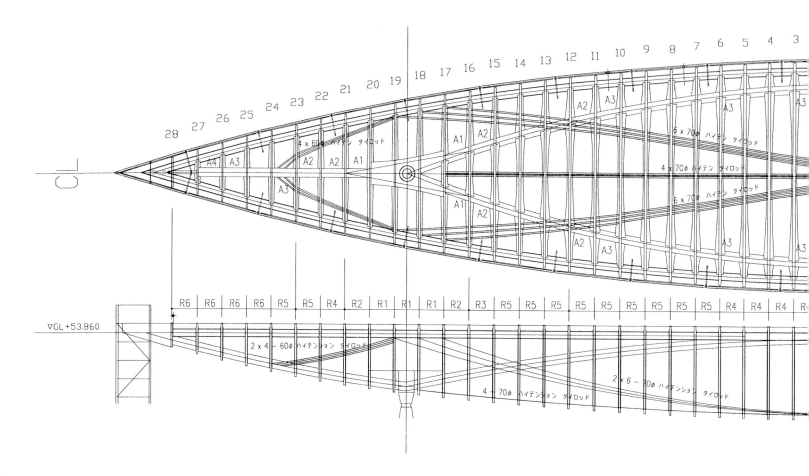

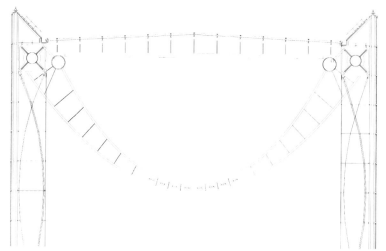

Cross section of the roof.

Two large pillars with a maximum
diameter of 4.5 meters support the
great roof skeleton.

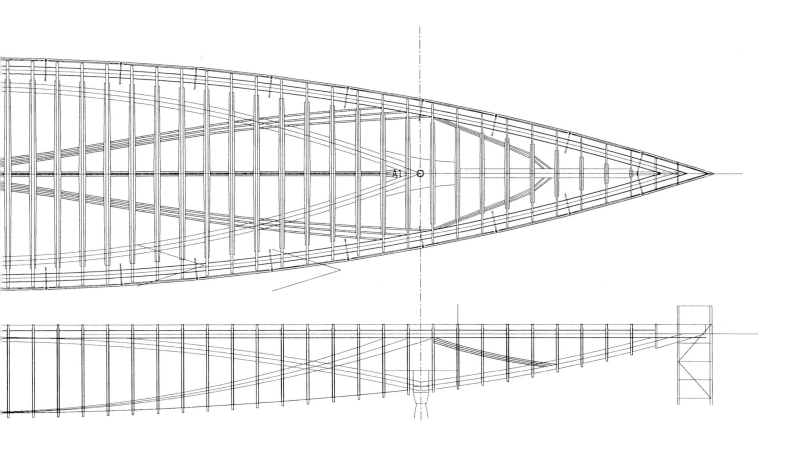

Organization of the atrium's covering structure.

The roof extends 124 meters
from one end of the atrium.

Secondary School in Utrecht

Erick van Egeraat

When the team headed by Erick van Egeraat was contacted in connection to this project, the building itself had already been designed by a different architect. This meant that rather than being commissioned to design a new building to be used by the secondary school for graphic and fashion design, the team was asked to intervene on an existing project with a view to obtaining the approval of the region's so-called Aesthetic Committee.

The committee consisted of a group of historians, architects, and politicians responsible for assessing the quality and design suitability of the projects to be built in each area. This important administrative juncture, which involved potential objections and complications due to the subjective nature of the committee, was what made it necessary to give Van Egeraat and his team of collaborating architects the opportunity to participate.

The commission's main stipulation was to revitalize the image of the other architect's project and, secondly, to replan the entrance foyer. With the aim of giving new

Location: *Utrecht, Holland.*
Date: *1994-1997.*
Client: *Utrecht City Council.*
Collaborators:
Maartje Lammers,
Ard Buijsen, Boris Zeisser.
Structure: *Strukton*
Engineering b.v, Maarsen.
Installations: *Sweegers & de*
Bruijn b.v, Den Bosch.
Subcontract for the façade:
Rollecate, Staphorst.
Program: *Secondary school*
for graphic and fashion design.

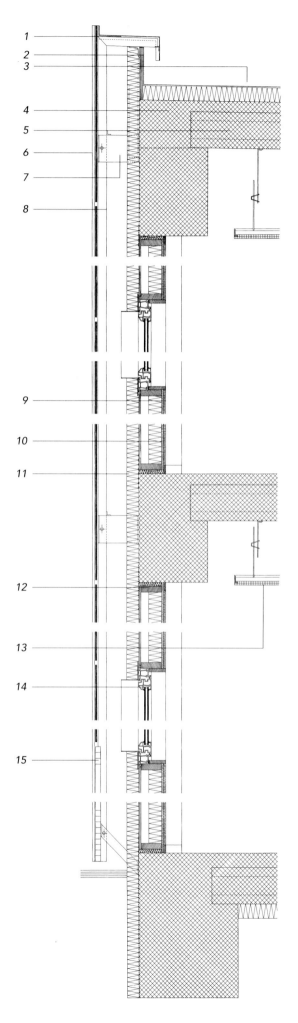

Vertical working section of the façade.

1. Aluminum sheet.
2. Compressed wooden strip.
3. Protective roofing felt.
4. Concrete.
5. Prefabricated wall elements.
6. 8 mm transparent glass.
7. Anchorage.
8. Aluminum frame.

9. 2 x10 mm plaster board panels.
10. Steam barrier.
11. 75 mm thermal insulation.
12. 12 mm compregnated wooden strip.
13. False ceiling.
14. Aluminum frames.
15. Steel framework.

To completely transform the building's image, a second, glass skin is superposed on the existing façade, which was designed by a different team of architects.

View from inside the foyer, also part of this design project. In the background, the glass skin remains at the same level, though the existing building decreases in height.

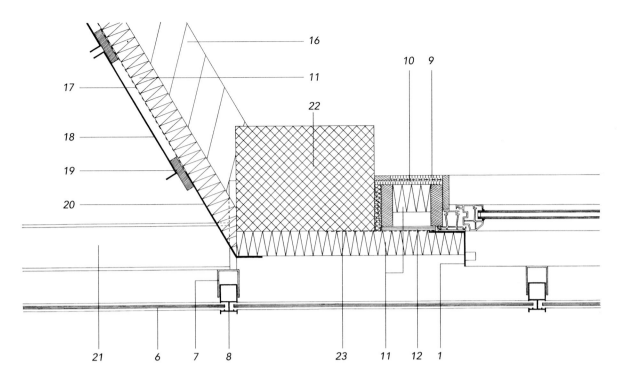

Horizontal working section of the façade where it meets the entrance foyer.

16. Masonry.

17. Asphalt material.

18. Interior cladding.

19. Wooden rails.

20. Galvanized steel plate.

21. HEB 140.

22. Concrete pillar.

23. Asphalt material.

General view from the patio. The second skin, designed by Van Egeraat's studio, stands independently of the existing volume.

life to an inert volume, without leaving scars or doing violence to the structure, the architects chose to design an independent glass skin which they superposed on the existing façade. This skin swathed the building in a kind of veil that shows it off and at the same time transforms the viewer's perception of what lies behind. The fact that this new skin is completely independent, placed over an existing building, is stressed at each possible point. Glass is used as a filter; its transparency provides an image of what lies behind and overlaps with it, clinging to it like a reflection. Beneath the glassy skin comes the next layer, now clad with three different materials: pine, brick and thermal insulation.

The replanning of the entrance foyer, at one of the corners between two blocks, brought about a radical change in concept. The foyer houses the main hall, seen

Ground plan of the site.
Uses are in accordance
with the urban design
plan for the area.

1. School.
2. School..
3. Housing.
4. Existing buildings.

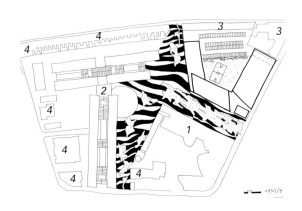

The use of glass is carried to the
ceiling of the foyer, which houses an
independent volume intended for the
conference hall, reception, and
suspended walkways communicating
the upper levels.

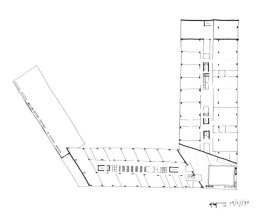

Second floor.

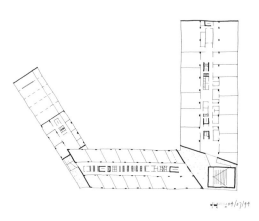

First floor.

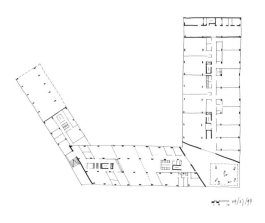

Ground floor.

as a completely transparent volume, suspended on slender metal columns, and which almost seems to disappear. It also houses the reception and two walkways to connect the two wings at the different levels.

The use of glass is extended inside with the walkways, skylights, and façades, seeming to build one reflection upon another. The corrugated polycarbonate used for the volume of the main hall introduces the concepts of translucence and play of light. The installation of fluorescent lights on it are the work of minimalist artist Dan Flavin. The general concept for the foyer is that of volumes suspended in a space defined by a glass skin, a reference to the Faculty of Economics, also in Utrecht, and designed by Mecanoo, of which Erick van Egeraat was a founding member in 1983 and was the principal architect until 1995.

Pachinko Parlor II and III

Kazuyo Sejima

Pachinko is an extremely popular game in Japan, and one which combines chance with skill. There are amusement arcades all over the country with almost identical layouts: rows and rows of individual game machines. It was one client, the Kinbasha chain, which commissioned Kazuyo Sejima's team with three projects; we present the last two here, not only because they involve similar buildings, but also for certain approaches they have in common.

Pachinko Parlor II is a small intervention on a modest building in Naka, a provincial city an hour-and-a-half away from Tokyo by train. The building stands on a freeway, and is devoid of charms of any kind. The aim was to create an entrance which would attract the attention of both the pedestrian and drivers passing on the freeway at high speed. Into the 4.5 meters separating the building from the freeway, a glass box was introduced, measuring 42.5 meters in length and 4.8 meters high; this was to be the entrance hall and rest lounge for players taking a break. The freestanding façade consists only of great glass panels which repeat the name of the establishment, with the purpose of advertising it from a distance.

Pachinko Parlor II

Location: *Naka, Ibaraki, Japan.*

Date of completion: *1993.*

Structures: *Matsui Gengo & O.R.S.*

Brief: *Entrance Hall.*

Built surface area:
165 square meters.

Pachinko Parlor III

Location: *Hitachiohta,*
Ibaraki, Japan.

Date of completion: *1996.*

Structures: *Matsui Gengo & O.R.S.*

Brief: *Pachinko Parlor.*

Built surface area:
800 square meters.

Pachinko Parlor II.

Previous page.
Pachinko Parlor III.

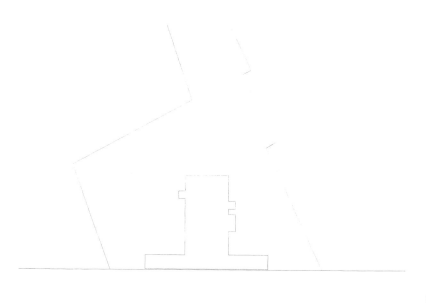

Pachinko Parlor II.
Inside the entrance hall.

Pachinko Parlor II.
Floor plan and location.

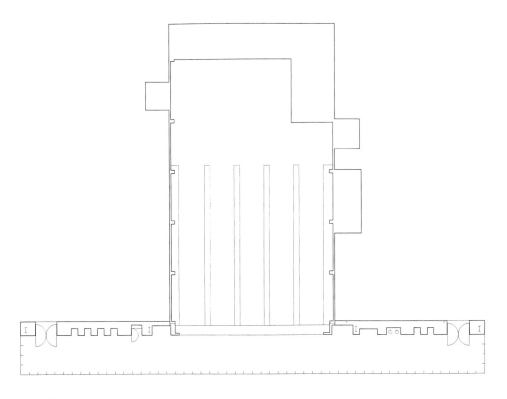

Pachinko Parlor II.
Floor plan.

A yellow wall provides the backdrop to the glazed surface, housing the entrance hall's ventilation shafts, as none of the panels open. This space is the entrance hall, so its long wall is interrupted by vending machines. The letters engraved on the glass merge in with the reflections of the sky, trees and movement of traffic during the day, and the neon lights, billboards and car head lamps at night.

Pachinko Parlor III followed number II. It is also in a provincial city, Hitachiohta, occupying a large site adjacent to a freeway. It has the typical neighbors of any provincial suburb, where cubic volumes, all alike, try to distinguish themselves with large signs announcing the companies they accommodate. Each volume is planted square in the middle of its site, forming strange archipelagoes. This small building occupies just 700 square meters of the 4,000 square meters available.

This particular option was governed by the desire to keep some distance, yet without really wanting to stand apart from its neighbors. The layout in rows of

Pachinko Parlor II. Reflections, like the letters, adhere to the glass, creating a constantly changing appearance.

Pachinko Parlor II. Inside the entrance hall, showing the frameless glass walls.

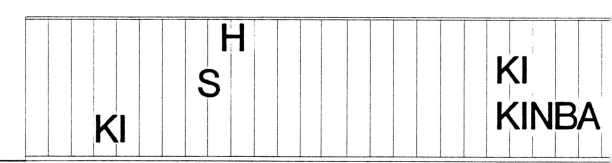

pachinko machines provided the clue to a volume in keeping with the activity going on inside: basically rectangular, and curving to follow the line of the freeway which it borders.

The curvature of the façade and the use of light and materials were quite notorious enough to require just a humble sign to announce the name of the establishment, in which glossy black strips frame colored glass fragments. During the day, the black gloss smoothly returns reflections while at night, the light inside the building sees these strips disappear to become a framework which marks out the facade.

The first floor is a typical pachinko hall with rows of machines, prize-winners' corner and a lounge for resting. The office is separated from the other spaces, being located beneath a gently curving slab. The slope of the floor adds to the charm of the rest lounge, overlooking the gaming room. The entrance way, which is also sloping, leads into the hall at the point of inflection of the curved slab.

Pachinko Parlor II.
Elevations.

Pachinko Parlor II.
Elevation by night and day.

Pachinko Parlor III.
Exterior of the southeast façade.

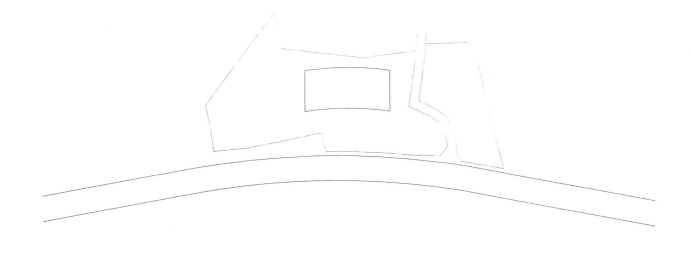

Pachinko Parlor III.
Floor plan of location.

Pachinko Parlor III.
Outside, during the day.

Pachinko Parlor III.
The façade, seen
from the inside.

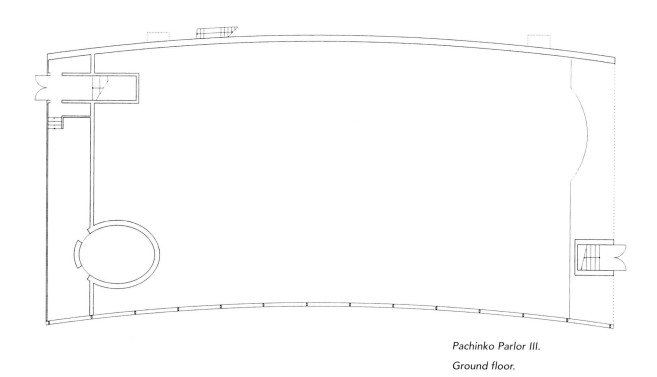

Pachinko Parlor III.
Ground floor.

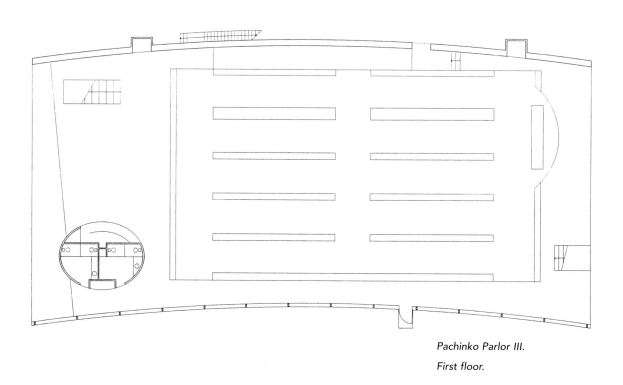

Pachinko Parlor III.
First floor.

Pachinko Parlor III. View of
the rest lounge.

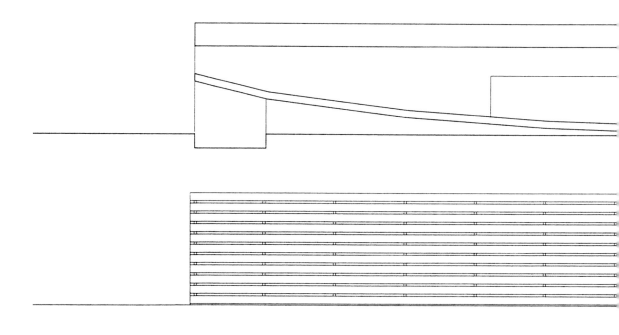

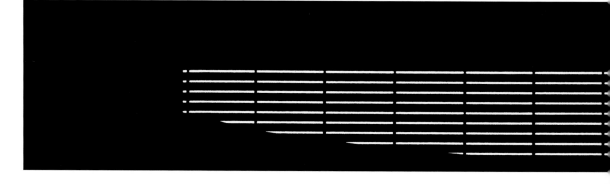

Pachinko Parlor III.
Entrance hall.

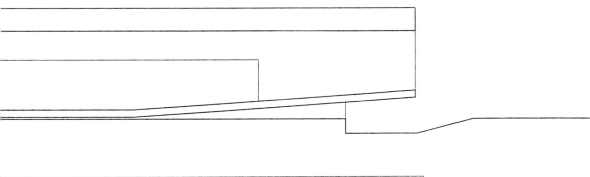

Pachinko Parlor III.
Longitudinal section.

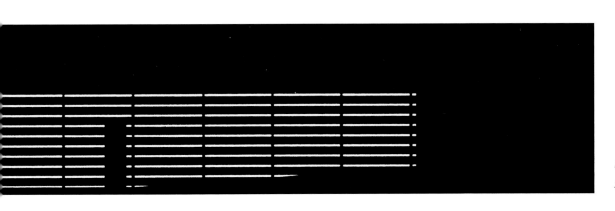

Pachinko Parlor III.
Southeast elevations.

Le Palais des Beaux-Arts de Lille

Jean Marc Ibos and Myrto Vitart

At the end of the 1980s the Musée des Invalides in Paris offered to donate their collection of relief plans (the word model was not used in the 17th century) of the cities and fortresses in the Lille area made by the strategists of Louis XIV to the Palais de Beaux-Arts. This led to a project for the complete renovation of a building that a century of bureaucratic mangagement had left in a deplorable architectural state. The arcades giving access to the atrium or interior patio which at one time was the organizing point of the routes that traverse the interior exhibition rooms had been walled up. Stairs and offices had been added which covered up the domes above the different wings. The successive changes meant that the building had become isolated from the Place de la République, which connects it to the center of the city.

However, the bases of the competition convoked in 1990 contemplated not only the renovation of the existing building and its adaptation to current standards, but the possibility of a complete rethinking of the way the existing collections were exhibited. In addition, there were to be new rooms

Location: *Lille, France.*

Dates: *march, 1990 (contest);*
1990-1992 (preliminary planning);
1992-1997 (construction).

Client: *Lille City Council.*

Associates: *Pierre Cantacuzène, coordinator,*
Sophie Nguyen, façades of the
palace and museography.

Structure: *Ingeniería Khephren.*

Installations: *Ingeniería Alto.*

Façades: *Y. R. M. Antony Hunt &Ass.*

Program: *Renovation and new construction of*
permanent and temporary exhibition rooms and
of areas housing the services of the museum.

Surface area: *28,000 square meters total,*
of which 11,000 square meters
are of new construction.

View from the Palais de Beaux-Arts de Lille, looking towards the new screen/building.

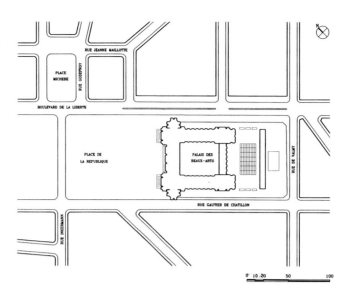

Site plan, showing the structuring function acquired by the patio or atrium of the Palais in linking the Place de la République with the new glass structure.

Detail of the reflection of the Palais caught in the north façade of the new building-screen. The glass is engraved with a series of tiny mirrors, giving this impressionistic, almost pointillistic image. The superimposition of this plane and the panels chromed in gold and red which lies behind interplays with the silhouette of the shadow projected by the Palais.

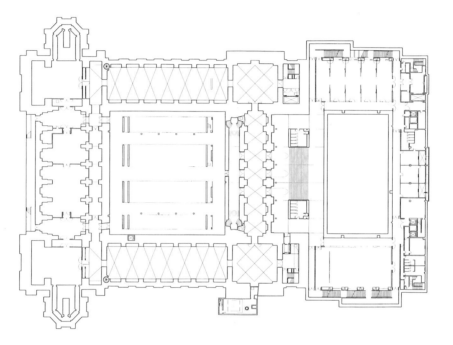

Plan of the first underground level, with the temporary exhibition rooms under the horizontal glasswork and the relief plans on exhibit under the atrium. Also showing how the Palais and the new conservation workshops are connected.

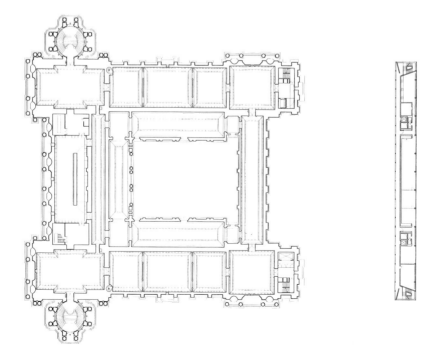

Plan of the first floor of the Palais, which corresponds to the third floor of the building-screen. This building is representative of a solemn architecture of mass, shadows, and light, with a spatial luxury that is inconceivable in our times, and with majestic volumes and beautiful perspectives.

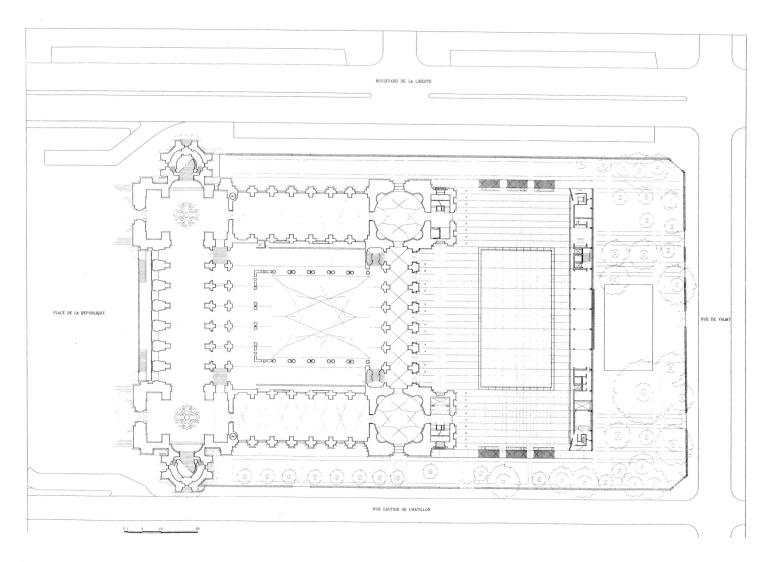

BOULEVARD DE LA LIBERTE

PLACE DE LA REPUBLIQUE

RUE DE VALMY

RUE GAUTIER DE CHATILLON

0 1   5   10   20

for housing the collection of relief plans as well as the construction of a room for temporary exhibitions, an auditorium, a library, and educational workshops. Also planned was the reorganization of the museum´s conservation service with the creation of new technical workshops. In all, it was envisaged that about 5,000 square meters of exhibition space would be added to the existing 17,000 square meters.

The Palais was constructed in 1895 and was a reduced version of a more ambitious design by Berard and Delmas in the style of the Musée du Louvre. The original plan called for a building twice the built size. This would have filled the site now occupied by the new construction of Ibos and Vitart, the winners of the modern competition. Ironically, these architects have chosen to use a glass building-screen that reflects the old palace, doubling its

image, and thereby redeeming the idea of the original design.

"We wanted to go towards the meaning of the building, with the idea of taking advantage of its qualities," explain the architects in the memorandum of the plan for the renovation and enlargement of the Palais. This philosphy impregnates each decision taken, such as tearing down all the additions such as dividing walls, false ceilings, improvised service stairs and restoring or reinforcing the views in depth which were thus revealed. In the same line, the atrium was opened up to become a meeting and transit point and a route was established leading from the Place de la République, through the atrium and the ground floor of the new building where the café-restaurant is housed, to the sculpture garden which abuts Rue Valmy at the southern boundary of the site.

Ground floor. Both of the rotundas nearest to the glassed plaza are almost completely filled by the enormous chandeliers by Pesce. The Palais is entered from the Place de la République.

Cross section AA-AA'of the Palais
through the atrium which the renovation
has turned into a covered plaza.

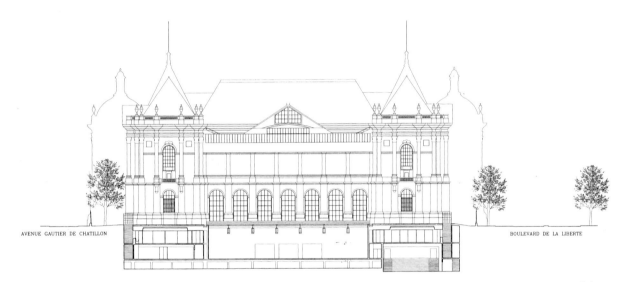

Cross section AC-AC'of the
temporary exhibition rooms. The six
main beams of the glass roof are
aligned on the axes of the arcades of
the façade of the Palais.

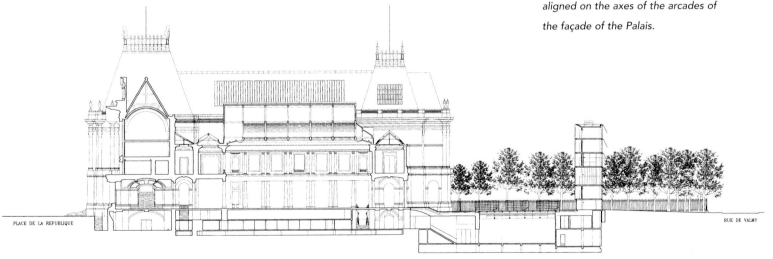

Longitudinal section AB-AB'. The
difference in ground level between the
atrium and the new glazed space creates
a succession of reflections which a level
site would have rendered imperceptible.

Excavation of the floor beneath the atrium liberated a large space which was used to house the new collection of "relief plans". The size of the space is to the scale of the models on view, some of which are more than 150 square meters. The walls, floors, and ceiling are black and the light perfectly catches the exactitude of the bas-relief work, enabling the collection to be viewed optimally.

Undoubtedly, one of the most important elements in the interplay of perspectives and reflections is the new building-screen, and the false pond, also made of glass, which opens and closes electronically and forms the roof of the new room for temporary exhibitions. It is placed strategically between the original building and the building-screen which catches the reflection of the former, evoking the memory of the original Berard and Delmas design.

In the south façade, a system of sensors measures the direct sunlight, the temperature, and the wind speed and automatically controls a system of external awnings. The special feature of the horizontal glass which forms the false pond is the slightness of its inclination (1%) and the dimensions of its glass panels which measure 5450 x1900 mm each. The panels are supported by a network of steel profiles, in turn supported by six 19-meter steel beams, which cross the room on its short side. Between the beams, another automated system controls the sunlight and adapts the level of natural light to the requirement of the works on exhibition. The beams are covered with aluminum sheets and the resulting space contains the air conditioning and artificial lighting.

View of the atrium, with the glass cubes by Paolini.

The wing dedicated to paintings
in the Palais de Beaux-Arts.

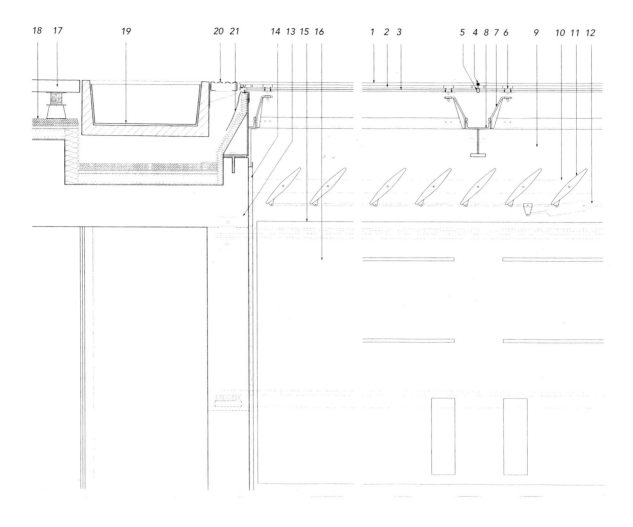

Longitudinal section of the horizontal glasswork.

1. Climalit, 15 mm.

2. Air chamber, 15 mm.

3. Tempered laminated glass,
   10/10/4 mm.

4. Joint of black silicone.

5. Frame of medium density polyethylene
   which complements the waterproofing
   of the silicone joints, carrying any
   infiltrating moisture to the
   UPN 150 profiles which act as gutters.

6. Swivel.

7. Clamps of laminated steel which are
   joined to the UPN 150 profile by bolts.

8. UPN150 soldered over sheets of
   laminated steel.

9. Steel underpinning.

10. Profile of gray-lacquered steel supports.

11. Open silver blinds.

12. Electric jack, elevated.

13. Concrete structure.

14. Plaster facing.

15. 3 mm steel sheathing of the
    main beams.

16. Main beam of steel.

17. Polished concrete slab.

18. Combination of isolation and waterproofing.

19. Polished concrete basin.

20. Grating of stainless steel.

21. Medium density polyethylene
    waterproofing.

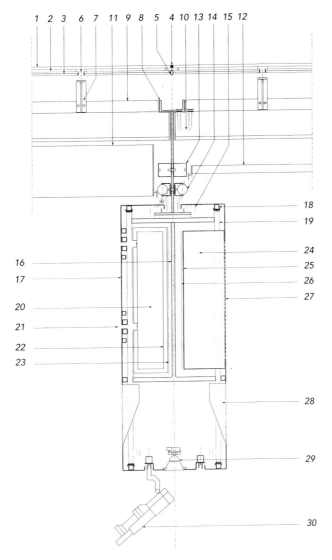

1 2 3 6 7 11 9 8 5 4 10 13 14 15 12

18
19
24
25
26
27

16
17
20
21
22
23

28

29

30

Transversal section of the horizontal glasswork.

1. Climalit, 15 mm.

2. Air chamber, 15 mm.

3. Tempered laminated glass,
   10/10/4 mm.

4. Joint of black silicone.

5. Frame of medium density polyethylene.

6. Swivel.

7. Laminated steel clamp joined to
   the UPN 150 profile by bolts.

8. UPN 150 soldered onto laminated
   steel sheets.

9. UPN 150 soldered onto
   steel underpinning.

10. Bridging element

11, 12. Silver blinds in open and
   closed positions.

13. Gray-lacquered steel profile
   supporting the blinds.

14. Electric jack, elevated.

15. Conduit box.

16. Main beam of steel.

17. 3 mm steel sheathing of the
   main beams.

18. Steel tubing 30x30x2 mm.

19. Steel tubing for support 50x30x2 mm.

20. Air conditioning conduit.

21. Lineal diffuser.

22. Fiberglass, 25 mm.

23. Protective sheathing.

24. Ventilation conduit.

25. Steel sheeting, 3 mm.

26. Protective sheathing 4 mm.

27. 30% perforated sheeting, 3 mm.

28. Ipso adjustable lamp.

29. Erco low-voltage embedded
   halogen light.

30. Very low-voltage projector with
   shutter framing, mounted on rails.

Previous page.

Detailed view of the horizontal glasswork from the temporary exhibition room.

Detail of the resolution of the north façade, seen from the corridor of the building-screen.

View of the horizontal and north façade glasswork of the building-screen.

The south façade of the building-screen and the sculpture garden, seen from Rue Valvy, showing clearly the shade of red that characterizes the whole project.

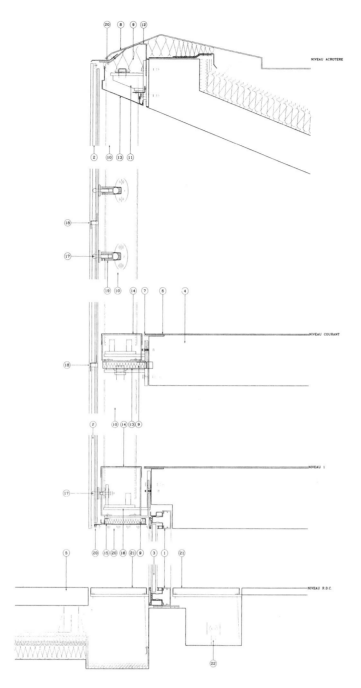

NIVEAU ACROTERE

NIVEAU COURANT

NIVEAU I

NIVEAU R.D.C.

Section of the north façade of the new building-screen.

1. Profile of aluminum.

2. Engraved Climalit glass, 10 mm;
   air chamber, 15 mm; tempered
   laminated glass, 66.4 mm.

3. Climalit, 88,2 mm.

4. Concrete panels, 230 mm.

5. Polished concrete slab, 80 mm.

6. PVC floor lining.

7. Metal border.

8. Cornice of Alucobond aluminum
   sheeting, 4 mm.

9. Mineral wool.

10. Elliptical ties of stainless steel
    which form the structural support
    of the façade between each level.

11. Plate fixing the tubing.

12. Galvanized steel sheeting, 30/10.

13. Steel sheeting 20/10.

14. Grating of stainless steel.

15. Galvanized steel sheeting 20/10.

16. Plate of galvanized steel, 10 mm.

17. Articulated anchor bolt fixing
    the glass panel.

18. Joint of black silicone,
    double barrier.

19. Fixing bolt of stainless steel.

20. Joints of black medium density
    polyethylene.

21. Grating of stainless steel.

22. Conduction tube.

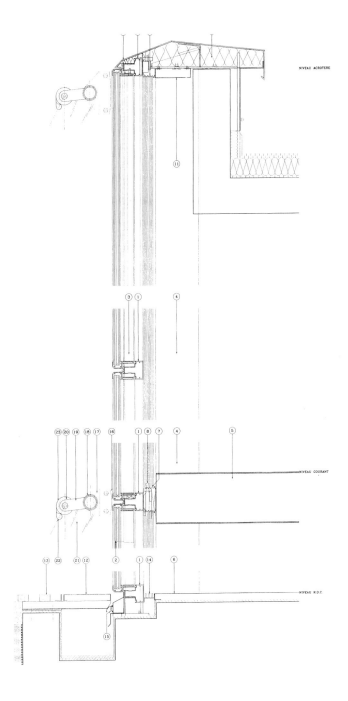

Section of the south façade of the screen/building.

1. Profile of aluminum.
2. Matrix glass, 4 mm;
   Planitherm sheet, 6 mm;
   air chamber, 10 mm;
   reeded glass, 6 mm.
3. Aluminum tie.
4. Concrete pillar.
5. Concrete panel, 230 mm.
6. Layer of cement.
7. Expansion joint of black medium
   density polyethylene.
8. Regulating screw.
9. Cornice of aluminum sheeting,
   Alucobond, 4 mm.
10. Mineral wool.
11. Galvanized steel sheeting 20/10.

12. Grating of stainless steel.
13. Curbing.
14. Ventilation grate of aluminum.
15. Self-regulating grate.
16. Stainless steel plate supporting
    the exterior awnings, 8 mm.
17. Stainless steel plate, 8 mm.
18. Support tube of stainless steel,
    diameter 70 mm, 4 mm.
19. Plate of stainless steel, 8 mm.
20. Motor tube.
21. Arm of the awning.
22. Load-bearing bar of stainless steel,
    diameter 25 mm.
23. Strengthened fabric of white PVC.

Galeries Lafayette

Jean Nouvel

This is a building for a typical urban, fairly diverse purpose, which includes the shopping mall for the Galeries Lafayette as well as spaces for offices, shops, apartments, and car parking. The chosen site occupies more than half a block in the cultural center of Berlin, right beside Schinkel's Schauspielhaus, with its great volume presenting three façades to the street and one backing onto neighboring buildings. The main street of the three is Friedrichstrasse, with Französischestrasse and Jägerstrasse being the two side streets. The volumetry of the block allowed construction of up to seven stories, in addition to the four basement floors, and the building emerges two floors above the surrounding houses.

Nouvel designed a volume which is glazed on all four sides (including the roof) to allow the interactive play of the daylight outside, the light shining in, and the artificial light generated by the building itself. The overall effect of the reflections creates an atmosphere which is both spectacular in that it responds to the characteristics of the activities going on within, and also clearly functional in that it does not cloud

Location: *Friedrichstadt Passagen Block 207, Friedrichstrasse – Französischestrasse, Berlin (Germany).*
Date of competition: *March 1991.*
Construction dates:
September, 1992 to March, 1996.
Client: *Euro-Projekt Entwicklungs GMBH.*
Architects responsible for the project:
Barbara Salin (competition phase), Laurence Daude (execution phase), Judith Simon, Viviane Morteau (works management).
Useful surface area:
39,585 square meters.

*The main inverted cone goes
down to the fourth basement.*

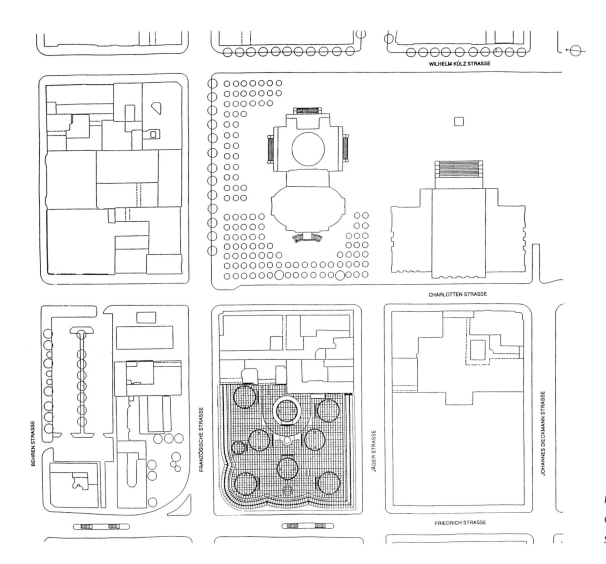

WILHELM KÜLZ STRASSE

CHARLOTTEN STRASSE

BEHREN STRASSE

FRANZÖSISCHE STRASSE

JÄGER STRASSE

JOHANNES DIECKMANN STRASSE

FRIEDRICH STRASSE

*Plan of situation. Behind the
Galeries to the right is
Schinkel's Schauspielhaus.*

the user-spectator's sense of orientation. The project's overall strategy addresses the recreation of the indoor-outdoor atmosphere of the 19th century's shopping arcades, with the public/semi-private ambiguity that made them the ideal link between commercial activities and city life in that century, while at the same time allowing the inhabitants a degree of interaction.

To achieve these aims, and given the dimensions of the volumes, Nouvel resorted to the strategy of perforating through the glazed body to generate multiple paths of light, all different, all organized according to a hierarchy. Almost all of these light wells adopt a conical geometry so that in all cases the activity on each level is different from the others. However, these cones, almost all inverted, are combined with upright cones, and interspersed with cylindrical patios of a more conventional

nature. In this way, the entire volume is run through with a multiplicity of vastly differing but clearly identifiable lighting references, creating an atmosphere which is free of historical or external references, while totally controllable in itself.

The main cone, which has the largest diameter, occupies the central area and lets light shine right into the ground floor, where another smaller, inverted cone carries it through to the four basement levels. This is the first element in the hierarchy and, as such, has a peculiar characteristic; it has reflecting surfaces, so that not only does light filter through to the various spaces, it also forms reflections due to the curved nature of the cone's surface.

Four inverted cones set at the four corners of the building also take light as far as the ground floor, where the vertex provides the close to a marked descending gradation.

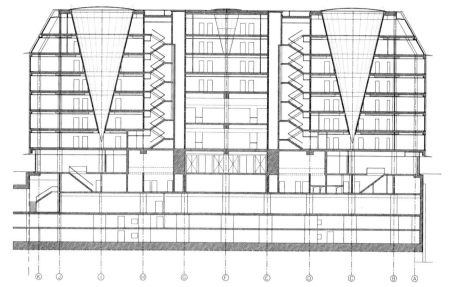

Section 7-7.

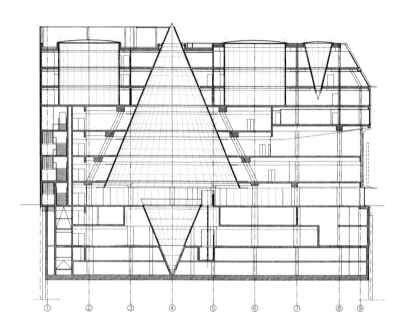

Section F-F.

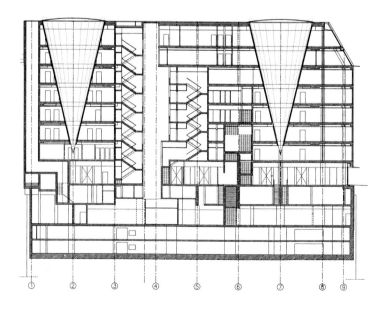

Section I-I.

View by night of the corner
of Friedrichstrasse and
Französischestrasse.

Along the façade on Friedrichstrasse, three huge screens project images onto the street, producing a new source of light which combines with the others to add to the light-filled complexity of the system without compromising its orderly interpretation.

In this solution for the Galeries Lafayette premises, Nouvel manages to combine the project's many underlying references: the geometric procedure is mindful of how the urban architecture of the last century resolved each specific problem arising from a particular site, almost in the same way that Schinkel applied his idea of hierarchy to the intricate plots of Berlin land, making the presence of the Schauspielhaus behind Nouvel's block seem something more than a coincidence. Ultimately, Nouvel has come up with a radical reply to the problem of chaos which normally exists in this type of space, by recourse to a solution which chooses to follow order and orientation. Providing an answer to the future urban life of Friedrichstrasse, Nouvel has compared his building to a great blaze of light "kindling one of the first fires of the rebirth of this street."

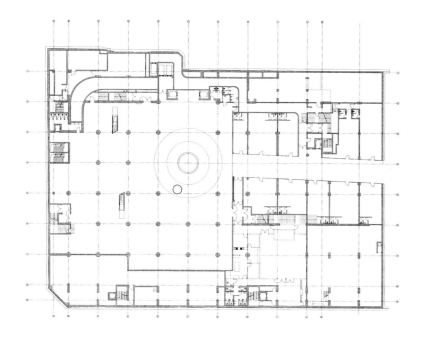

Second basement.

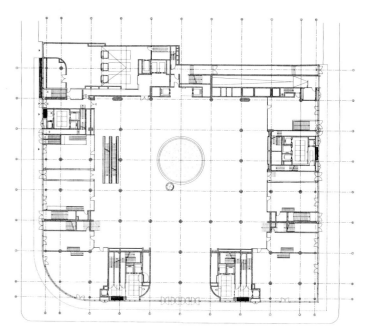

Ground floor (street level).

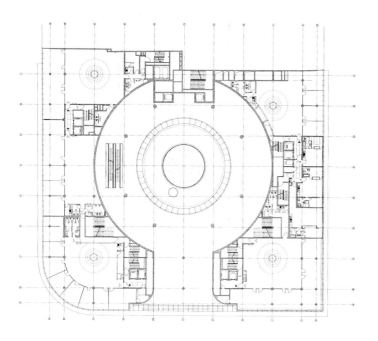

Second floor.

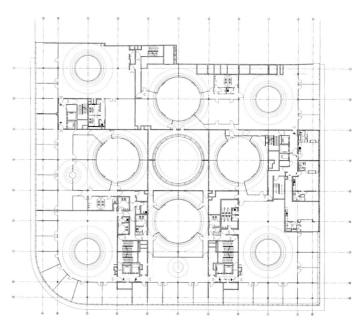

Fifth floor.

Detail of one of the inverted vertices.

The central cone, with the reflection on its inner surface.

Detail of the central cone.

The central cone reflects the inside, and its transparency provides a view of the city.

Overhead view of the central cone.

Lower vertex of one of the secondary cones.

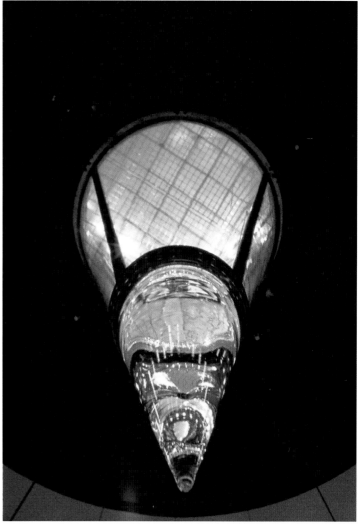

Behind the windows
of the attics.

The secondary cones
work as light patios.

View down through
one of the secondary cones.

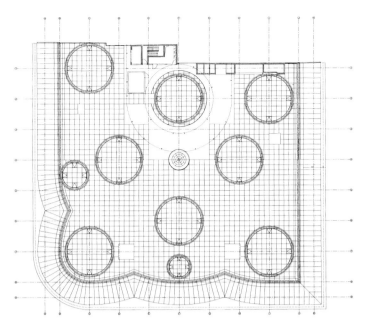

Plan of the roof.

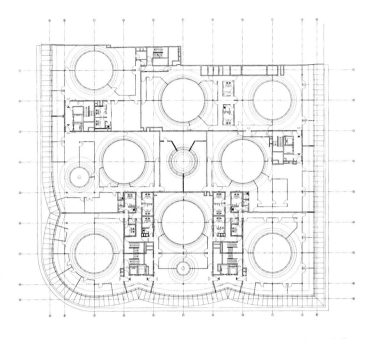

Seventh floor.

*Inside view of one of
the cylindrical patios.*

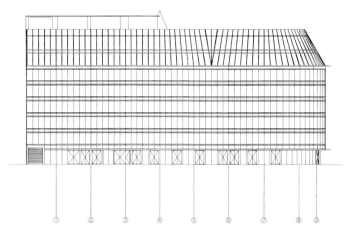

North façade (Französischestrasse).

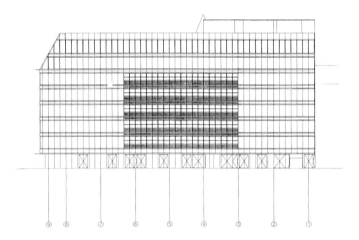

South façade (Jägerstrasse).

Façade on Jägerstrasse.

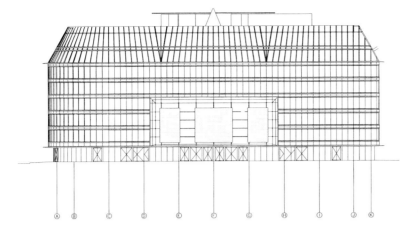

West façade (Friedrichstrasse).

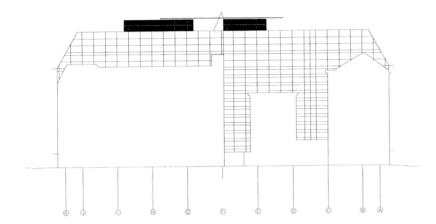

East façade (party wall).

Detail of the façade.

Façade on Friedrichstrasse.

Renovation and Enlargement of the Twenthe National Museum

Ben van Berkel

The Twenthe National Museum is located in Enschede, a regional capital. The original building was constructed in 1928 and occupies a large block. The building is almost symmetrical in shape, and consists of a complex of volumes parallel to the surrounding streets, which enclose a large central patio. Later enlargement added a second rectangle of blocks at the rear of the site, arranged around a somewhat smaller patio. The style is uniformly late Neo-Romanesque, with brick walls and steep roofs, although the planimetry of the complex brings to mind the 18th century.

The commission called for the covering of the rear patio, with the intention of using it as a new museum of modern art, and the construction of a new element to connect the museum with the larger patio. In addition, various specific additions such as new ramps and access stairs for the main entrance were to be carried out. All this implied a complete renovation of the interior of the building, with special emphasis on such elements as lighting, air conditioning, and heating.

The small glass and aluminum construction is designed to connect the museum

Location: *Lasondersingel 129-131, Enschede, The Netherlands.*
Date first phase:
November, 1995.
Date second phase:
March, 1996.
Client: Rijksgebouwendienst, Project Management, The Hague.
Builder: *Bouwbedrijf Punte bv, Enschede.*
Associates: *Harrie Pappot (Project coordinator), Joost Hovenier (Project manager).*
Landscape architect:
Lodewijk Baljon.

to the main patio. In his determination to reject any attempt at synthesis or dialogue with the original architecture, Van Berkel has positioned the new element at an angle to the axes of the old building, superimposing the new upon the old with total indifference. In reality, this construction, whose presence is so important in terms of effect, contains only an elongated services area and a multipurpose room. The design, however, is much more intentional than called for in the original project.

The interior shell, made of aluminum, is completely enclosed. By constrast, the outer shell is narrow and elongated and deliberately rejects any parallel with the inner shell in the design of its finish. The

roof inclines to one side and the horizontal walls finished with aluminum sheets follow this inclination. At one end the construction projects out over a small pond which occupies part of the patio. At the other end, the new body is supported by a plinth which elevates it off the ground. The entrance to the museum from the new structure is at an intermediate height and is reached by a ramp, thus further emphasizing the rupture with the ground.

The original commission called for this small pavilion to act as a viewing point of the main patio from the new museum. In fact, the view of the patio from the interior is limited by the architecture. The large inclined studs supporting the roof, the

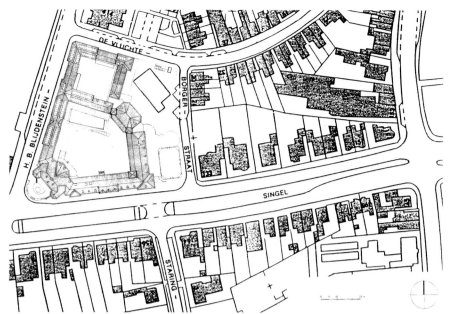

*Site plan of the Twenthe
National Museum.*

*Partial view of the small pavilion with the
old building in the background.*

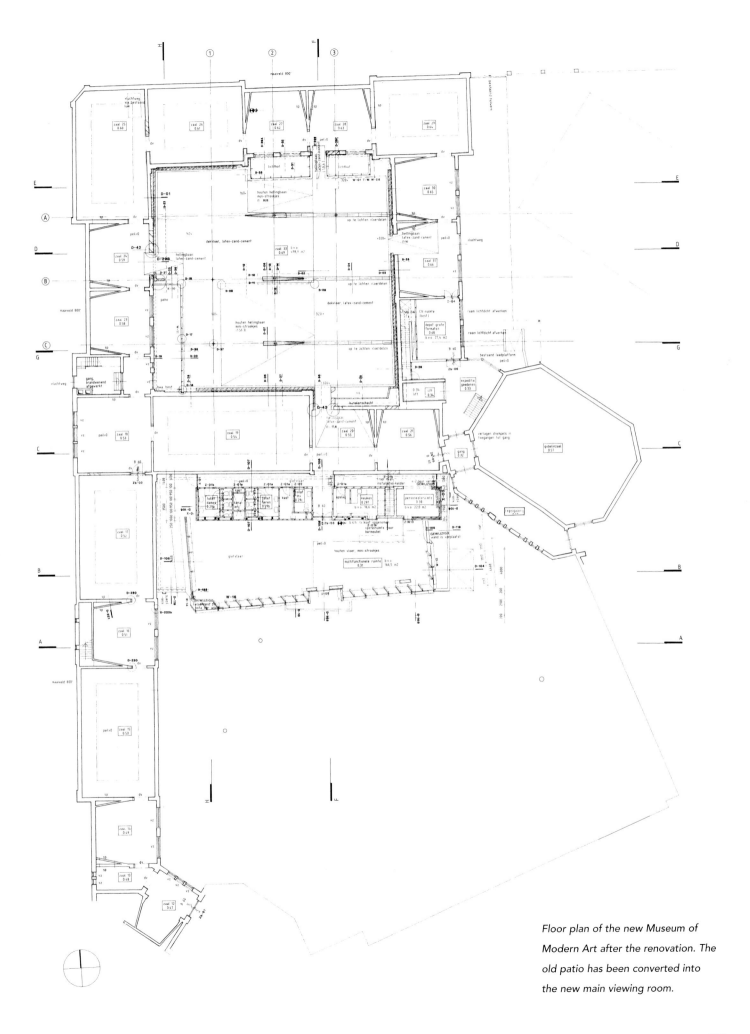

Floor plan of the new Museum of Modern Art after the renovation. The old patio has been converted into the new main viewing room.

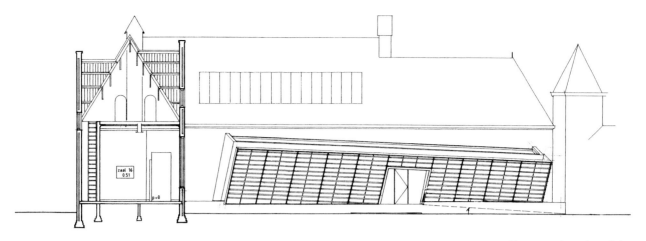

Transversal section of the main patio, with the elevation of the pavilion.

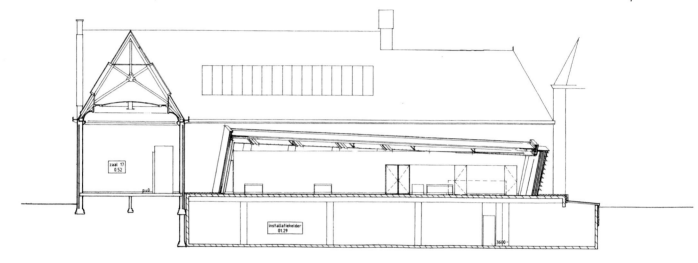

Longitudinal section of the pavilion.

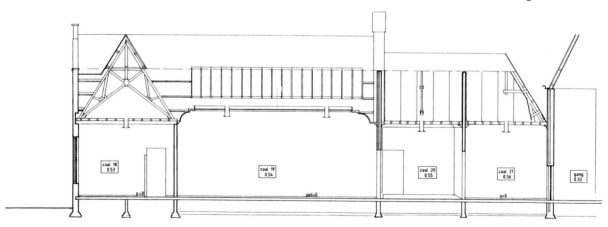

Longitudinal section of one of the wings of the museum.

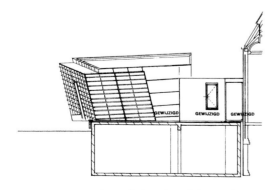

Lateral elevation of the pavilion destined as a multipurpose space.

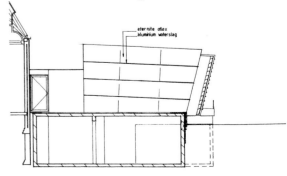

Lateral elevation of the pavilion at the end adjoining the old building.

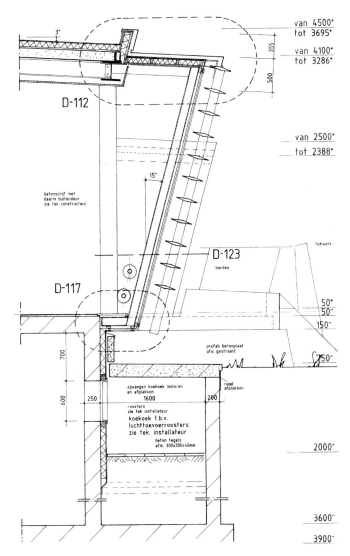

View of the main patio from the interior of the multipurpose space.

Detail of the finish of the multipurpose space. Section.

thick inclined sheets of aluminum and the twisted emplacement of the construction all act to severely impede the view of the exterior. By giving such importance to this small structure and by limiting the view of the patio from it, Van Berkel has evidently tried to establish a conflict with the original nature of the site he was called to work on.

In light of the new character assigned to the rooms intended for the museum of modern art, Ben van Berkel opted for a completely new atmosphere, achieved by radical transformations of the walls, floors, and ceilings. His first criterion was to take advantage of the building´s natural light. The spaces delimited by the old skylights became patios of light enclosed by screens of translucent glass, which in some cases do not extend to the floor, thereby leaving the old bricks below exposed to view. The translucent glass has the effect of orienting the vertical light outwards into the room evenly, while at the same time slightly changing its natural quality.

The high ceilings of the original design have been changed by the addition of false

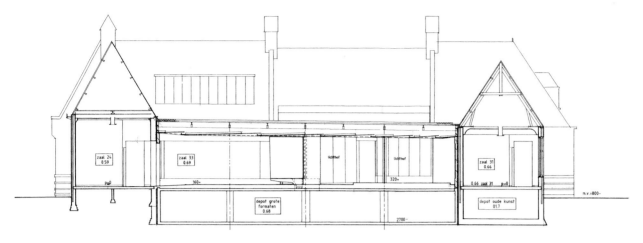

Cross section of the rear patio,
converted into the main exhibition
space of the new museum.

Longitudinal section, with the new
pavilion at the extreme right.

General view of the main
viewing room.

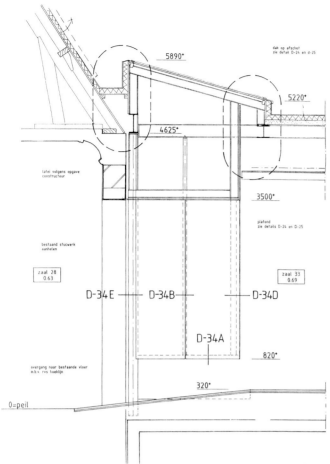

ceilings in all the new exhibition rooms. These combine opaque strips which accommodate the services, with strips of artificial light filtered by translucent glass that combines with the light from the small patios. The effect is to create an atmosphere where the sense of gravity becomes diffuse and vertical orientation is lost. The placing of the ceiling panels in inclined series gives a certain dynamism to the feeling of weightlessness, further heightened by the smooth inclination of the ramps which connect the rooms.

The original walls have been doubled by new concrete walls and these support

Detail of one of the glass patios under the skylights. The panels do not reach the floor.

In the foreground, the jutting block of concrete which supports the exhibition panels.

large white panels for exhibition purposes. In addition, new panels have been installed in the middle of the rooms, supported by a large piece of reinforced concrete which severs them from the floor and adds to the sense of weightlessness.

The new environment of the rooms is defined by the luminous panels of translucent glass, the wood of the carpentry and the ramps, the unadorned concrete of the structural elements, the white exhibition panels, and the smooth gray surface of the floors. This combination succeeds in erasing any trace of the original construction.

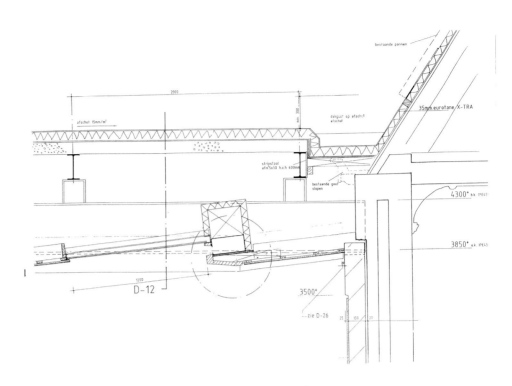

Detail of the false ceiling.

Warehouse for Ricola

Jacques Herzog & Pierre de Meuron

The new combined factory and warehouse of Ricola-Europe occupies a site in an industrial zone south of the city of Mulhouse in an area of great natural beauty in the forests of Alsace. The site itself is large and practically flat. The new building is a rectangular, easily recognizable single-story volume, almost symmetrical in form, and with a totally diaphanous interior.

Herzog and De Meuron solve the problem of the building's dual use as factory and warehouse by dividing it into ten bays of equal size. One partition runs longitudinally and is intersected by five transversal divisions. Each space has a centrally placed ventilation system which connects with the roof, ensuring that all parts of the building are ventilated equally.

The long sides of the rectangular building are dominated by huge identical canopies. Two large white signs bearing the logotype of the company are painted on the asphalt of the delivery service road. The two shorter walls of the building are flat planes of concrete with no openings, redeemed by the profiles of the two inclined canopies. The rainwater of the roof runs directly down the walls, creating a humid vertical plane providing ideal conditions for the climbing plants that are one of the most important features of the design.

Location: *Mulhouse, France.*
Date of design: *1992.*
Construction date: *1993.*
Client: *H.P. Richterich,*
Ricola AG, Laufen/CH.
Project manager:
André Maeder.
Landscape architect:
Dieter Kienast.
Polycarbonate panels:
Marc Weidmann.
Surface Area:
2,760 square meters.

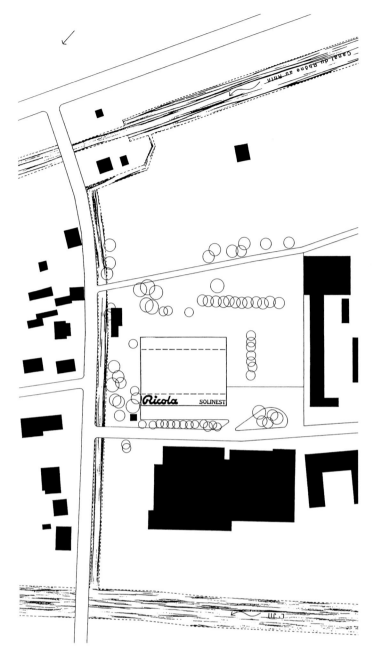

Location plan.

The façades of the two longer sides of the rectangle have been created by using undivided expanses of translucent polycarbonate, a common industrial material. These are covered by a serigraphed design of a plant which extends up to cover the canopies, as well. This innovative solution totally dominates both the exterior landscape appearance and the lighting of the interior. The polycarbonate is modified by the variations in sunlight and by the change between day and night. If the light is tenuous, the exterior material becomes more transparent, high lighting the serigraphy and creating the image of an engraving that simultaneously reflects, absorbs, and gives free passage to the light. However, if the outside light is more intense, the surface becomes more opaque, with greater reflective capacity, creating a dark plane where the drawings almost disappear and the image offered is more conventional. In this way, the skin of polycarbonate forms a heliotropical surface, receiving and reacting to the changes in sunlight, and defining the image of the building with relation to its immediate context.

The polycarbonate skin also has an important effect on the interior. The interior somewhat resembles an aquarium: immersed and somewhat separated from

*View of the façade used
for deliveries. Seen from
the access road.*

*General view of the
warehouse at night.*

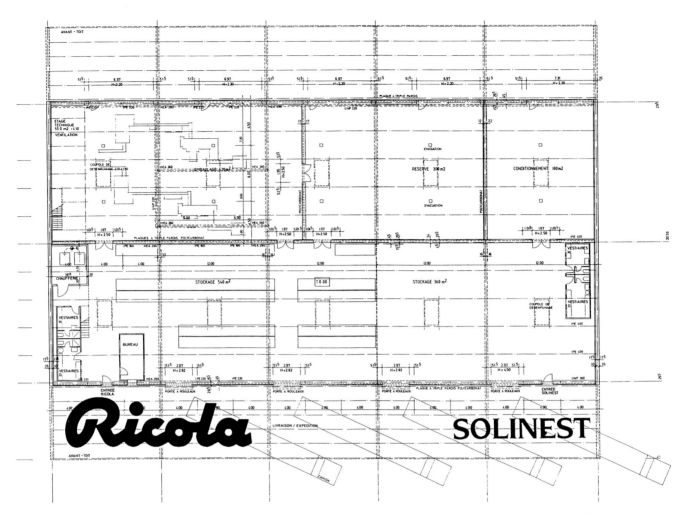

Floor plan of the warehouse.

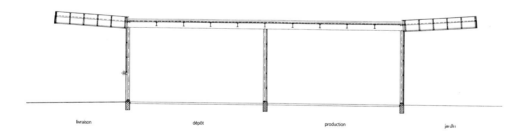

livraison   dépôt   production   jardin

*Cross section of the warehouse.
Loading and unloading.
Warehousing. Production.
Garden.*

the exterior. This separate interior landscape, conditioned by the changing nature of the translucent engraving throughout the day, maintains an indirect but real relationship with the beautiful forest landscape surrounding the building.

Herzog and De Meuron cleverly work with abstract elements in the landsaping of this building in order to establish a continuity with the natural features of the area. The overall design of the warehouse is strongly abstract, but the modules of the façade with the repeated plant motif is a form of using serialization and repetition to create an environment that, like nature itself, changes throughout the day. In effect, their design uses abstraction to create a natural world.

Detail of the façade from within,
looking out over the garden.

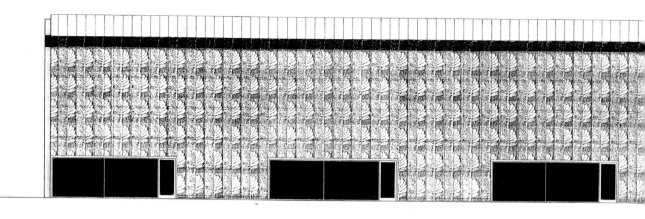

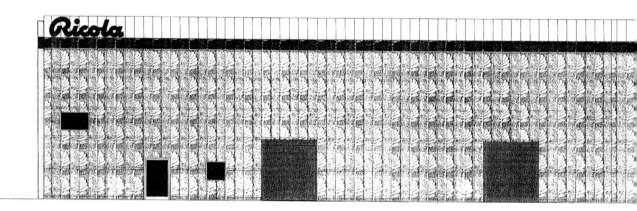

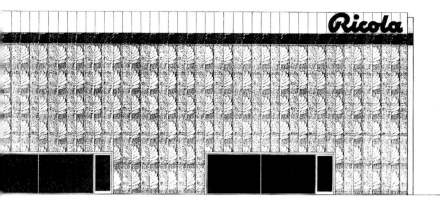

*Elevation of the
garden façade.*

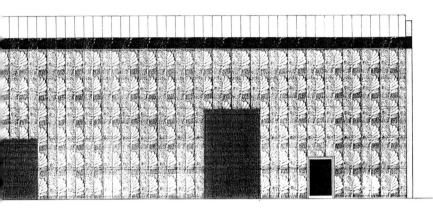

*Elevation of the façade used
for loading and unloading.*

Detail of the garden façade. The
serigraphs have disappeared,
obliterated by the reflected light.

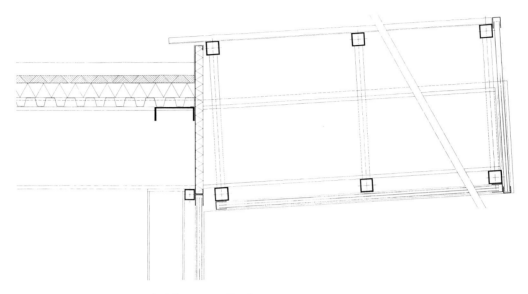

Detail of the canopy. Section.

Details of the façade. Ground plan and sections.

Detail of one of the
polycarbonate modules.

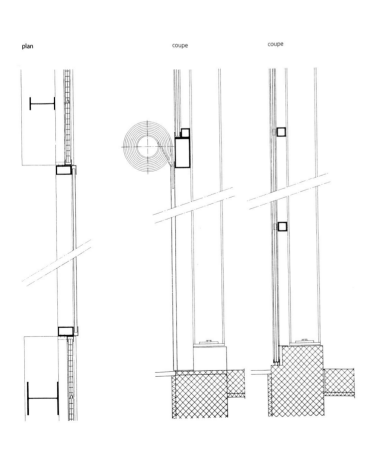

plan   coupe   coupe

Neanderthal Museum

Zamp Kelp
Julius Krauss
Arno Brandlhuber

The Neanderthal Museum holds the remains of Neanderthal man, the first of a series of primates with a skull similar in size to our own. The museum is located in the Neanderthal valley, near Düsseldorf, where the fossils were found in 1859. The exact site of the discovery, one of the caves in the valley's limestone quarry, was later destroyed by quarrying.

The museum complex consists of two independent buildings connected by an underground passageway. One of the buildings is dedicated to the administration and internal activities of the museum while the other holds the exhibitions, which consist not only of the fossils themselves, but also of several multimedia presentations spanning the entire history of human evolution.

The presentations are divided into five themes (Life and Survival, Technology and Knowledge, Myth and Religion, Environment and Food, and Language and Communication) and seven periods of time, ranging from four million years ago to the twenty-first century. These themes and periods of time mix and intertwine as the visitor advances toward the center of the museum.

Location: *Mettmann, Germany.*
Date: *1994-1996.*
Client: *Stiftung Neanderthal Museum ((Neanderthal Museum Foundation).*
Collaborators: *Thomas Gutt (coordinator), Astrid Becker, Marko Glashagen, Carlos González, Alex Kouzmine, Götz Leimkühler.*
Surface area:
2,800 m square meters.

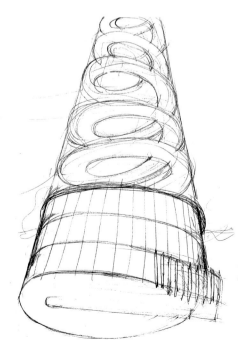
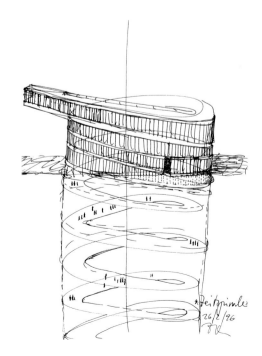

Northeast view of the
exhibition building.

The exhibition hall consists of three levels: the entrance, a lower level which houses the auditorium and rest rooms and connects the two buildings and an upper level with a cafeteria. A spiral ramp twists upwards through the museum.

The two buildings that make up the complex are different not only in function, but also in form. One of the most notable differences is in how the two structures are illuminated. The three-story administration building receives its light horizontally, through openings in the enclosing walls, whereas the exhibition section is lit from overhead by means of a skylight posi-

tioned over the stairs and placed in the center of the ramp to provide access to different points of the spiral.

From outside, the straightforward design of the administrative building contrasts with the paradoxical layout of the exhibition area. Whereas the former is illuminated through clearly visible openings in the façade, the latter presents the contradiction of a glass façade which corresponds to an opaque interior of polished concrete evoking a sense of the original cave where the fossils were found. The horizontal strips of glass on the outside also contrast with the total lack of horizontal planes on the

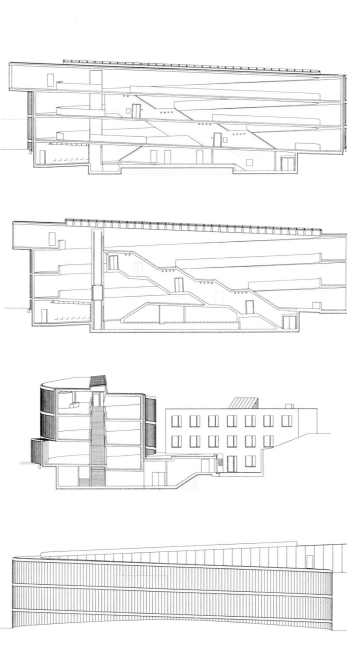

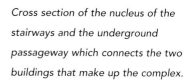

Longitudinal sections of
the ramp and stairways.

Cross section of the nucleus of the
stairways and the underground
passageway which connects the two
buildings that make up the complex.

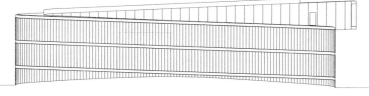

Northeast elevation.

Northwest elevation. The different
treatment given to the façades
of the two buildings reflects the
different functions of each:
administration and exhibition.

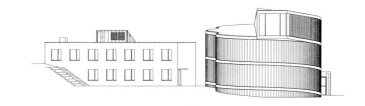

Southwest elevation.

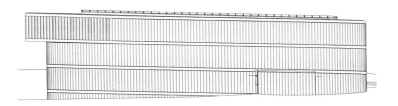

Southeast elevation. Both
buildings are located near one of
the sides of Neanderthal
valley, leaving maximum horizontal
space for the entrance.

Southwest view showing the glass enclosure between the end of the ramp and the cafeteria, which juts out from the exhibition area.

inside. In fact, the elevator near the stairs actually emphasizes the vertical direction.

As the author of the project points out, this paradox between the interior and exterior of the building originates from the contradictory conditions in which the museum took shape. The use of multimedia presentations and the eschewing of independent exhibition areas in favor of continuous development throughout the museum required a neutral, unobtrusive interior. On the other hand, the architect wanted the museum complex to take its place among the architectural landmarks and elements surrounding it on the highway between Düsseldorf and Mettmann, such as a square glass tower, a bridge across the highway, and a white silo that gives the impression of an acropolis.

In addition to these considerations, the choice of a spiral ramp as the main structuring element in the project has great symbolic value. The ramp acts as a symbol for the history of humanity, and when it ends at the cafeteria with an observation deck looking out over the valley, it invites us to reflect on the infinite scope of our journey through time. The wide open view before us reminds us that we are a part of the process, and that evolution does not end with us.

Seen in this light, the project plays a dual role: its glass shell makes it an architectural landmark, while its cavernous concrete interior provides a stage for an immersion in our past. The task of bringing the two together is carried out by the aluminum structure that supports the horizontal U-glass panels and the observation deck.

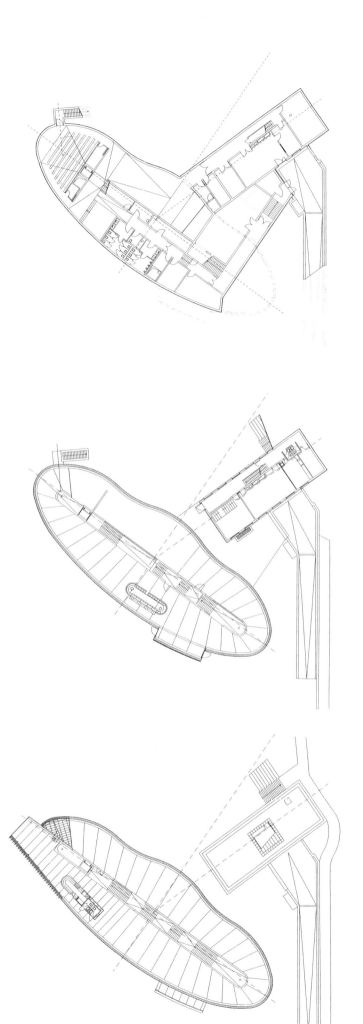

View of a point along the ramp.

Left.

The basement containing the auditorium and restrooms as well as the passageway which connects the administration and exhibition sections.

The ground floor, where independent access to both buildings is located.

Plan of the cafeteria and the roof of the administration building.

Entrance to the cafeteria,
with the gigantic observation
deck in the background.

The nucleus of the
ramp, containing the
stairs and elevator.

Southeast view of the entrance to the exhibition building.

Space between the administration and exhibition buildings.

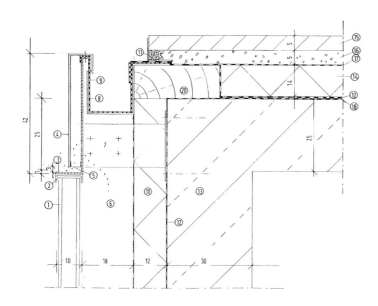

Detail of the enclosing crown.

1. U-glass panels (4 x 0.5 x 0.1 meters).	10. Thermal insulation (12 cm).
2. profile of aluminum framing for the panels.	11. Angle for gravel retention.
3. profile of laminated steel (400 x 70 mm).	12. Steam barrier.
4. Sheet of covering material.	13. Reinforced concrete.
5. Separator with insect-proof grid for the façade.	14. Fiberglass thermal insulation panels protected by bituminous exterior coating.
6. Air chamber (18 cm).	15. Concrete slab.
7. Profile of supports for laminated steel.	16. Gravel on separating sheet.
8. Drainage.	17. Two coats of waterproofing.
9. Waterproofing sheet for drainage.	18. Bituminous coating.
	20. Finishing board.

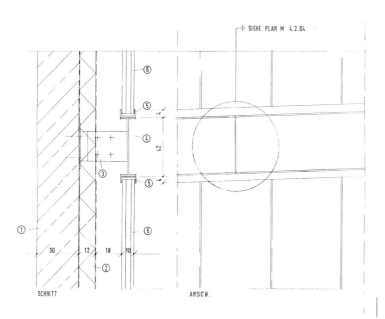

Detail of the façade covering.

1. Reinforced concrete wall.
2. Thermal insulation.
3. Stainless steel supports for the façade.
4. Profile of IPN (420 x 100 mm) for façade supports.
5. Profile of soldered aluminum.
6. Two U-glass panels with air chamber between them.

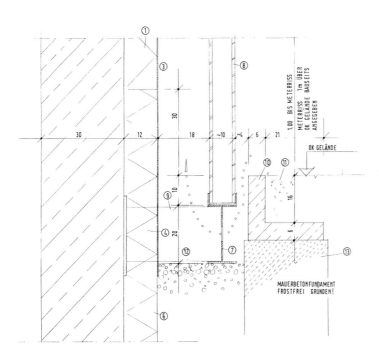

Detail of the foundation.

1. Thermal insulation (12 cm).	9. Stainless steel anchorage of the façade to the concrete wall.
3. 5% perforated aluminum sheeting.	10. Curb angle (6 cm).
4. Perimetric fiberglass socle with bituminous coating on both sides.	11. Soil filler.
6. Perimetric insulation (6 cm).	12. Gravel filler.
7. IPN profile of supports for U-glass panels.	13. Poured concrete foundation, placed over the ground, which is subject to freezing.
8. Façade of U-glass panels with air chamber between them, supported by aluminum UPN crossbeams and HEB stanchions.	

157

Electrical Grid Building

Mariano Bayón

Mariano Bayón's design for the Electrical Grid Building is a poetical interpretation of the forces of light. The building appears as a complex of four weightless walls lined with marble. However, the stone surface is so insubstantial that the light penetrates it, creating subtle nuances of luminosity.

Inside this skin of light, there is a juxtaposition of volumes within an empty space.

The architect offers a space which permits an encounter between the corporeal and the intangible: a void full of energy which gives meaning to the space. His objective is not to build, but to work with the positive and the negative, extracting another dimension from the materials.

The building has been designed to be seen at the entrance to the Expo, but not to be visited publicly. For this reason, it has been conceived as a box of light: an open box like a sculpture of translucent planes where the sun, the shadow, and above all the electric light produce the best effects. This gives the building two very different natures: opaque when the light is exterior and translucent when it comes from within. This effect is the result of using white marble cut into fine slabs, which gives a hard image by day, while throughout the night, the vision is warm and full of drawings and constant changes. The panels of marble are suspended over

Location: *Isla de la Cartuja, Seville, Spain.*
Date: *1991-1992.*
Client: *Red Eléctrica de España.*
Contractor: *Fomento de obras y construcciones.*
Associates:
F.J. de Mateo, Ulrich Nagel, Andreas Schwarz.

The stone surface is
penetrated by the light,
creating subtle variations.

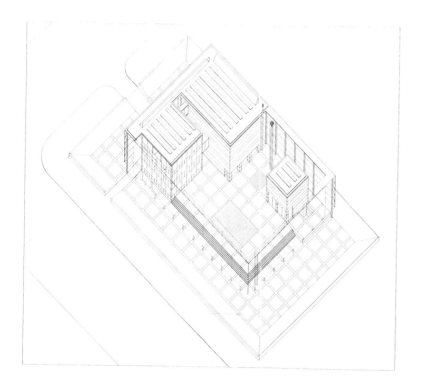

Axonometric view of the complex.

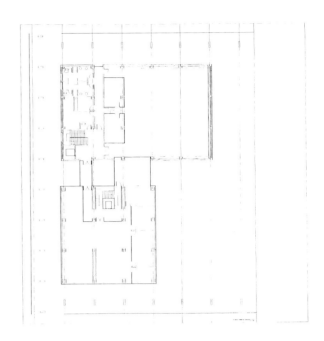

First floor.

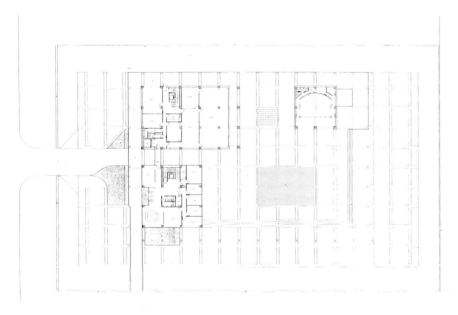

Floor plan.

a light structure hung from fine columns and do not reach the floor, acting almost as vertical blinds which allow the breeze to pass.

The four walls of marble filter the light of the interior which is inaccessable to the public. A basement floor contains the computers, the installations of the building and the general service areas. Above this, three parallelapipedic prisms serve to house the huge operations room for the Regional Center, with its screens; the

offices; and the zone of operations and maintenance. Two of the prisms are finished with white Macael marble and have a closed, compact look. The third has a tense skin of glass which lightens and elevates it.

In the patio, these three massive volumes are answered by a pond with fountains which pulverize the water, creating another volume which is almost immaterial, in homage to the prime material which is the source of so much electricity. The

placement of the three material volumes around the marble cuadrangle of the patio evokes Mies van der Rohe´s pavillions for Berlin and Barcelona: the patio-house, whose rooms here are the offices and operations areas of the building.

The design also contains constant references to Islamic architecture. Islamic art is an art of rest, more intellectual than emotional. The absence of tension is achieved basically by the subtlety of the surface

The building can be seen at the entrance to the Expo, but is not for public visits.

The box of light is
not closed, but open
like a sculpture of
translucent planes.

The interior, closed to
the public, appears as
a silent cloister
between the four veils
of white marble
which filter the light.

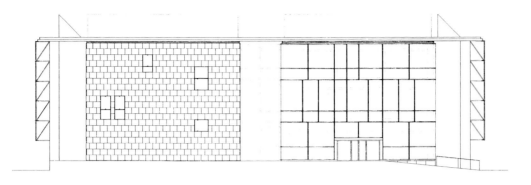

South elevation.

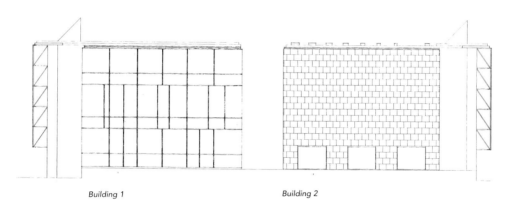

Building 1   Building 2

North elevation.

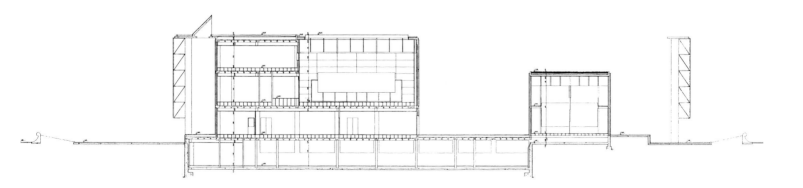

Longitudinal section.

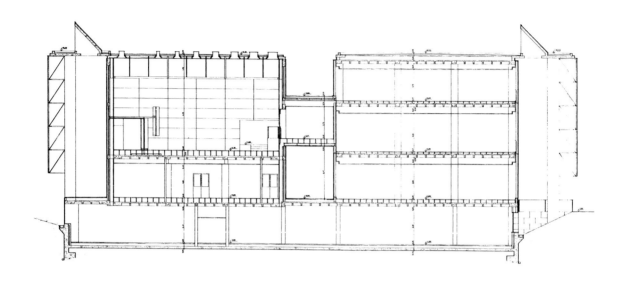

Transversal section.

decoration in which the drawings are limited to clearly defined zones, although at the same time they are infinite in the sense that they have unlimited possibilities of extension. The guiding principles are repetition and continuous permutation of motifs and designs. Like the water itself, which plays such a large role in the architecture, the decoration continually reflects its forms in order to provide a space that is "cold" to the gaze and to the spirit and creating an architecture that is dynamic but immutable.

Water and light are of primordial importance for Bayón and as in the architectural decoration found in Islam, they originate new layers of patterns and in this way transform the space.

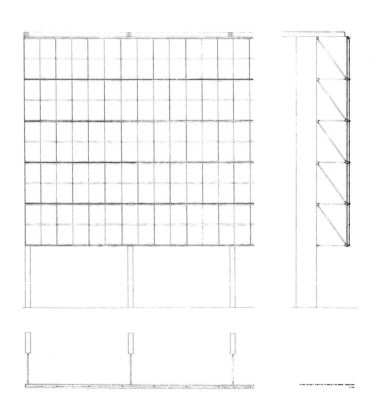

Elevation, section and floor plan of the screen of translucent marble.

Front elevation in daylight.

*The translucent walls,
hung from fine columns, do
not reach the ground.*

Two of the three prisms
which appear in the
patio are dressed with
white Macael marble.

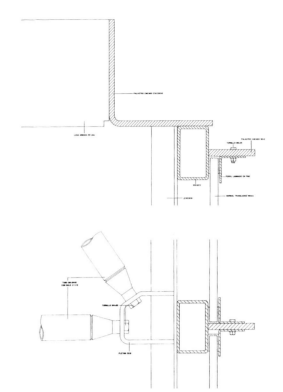

Constructive details of
the marble screen.

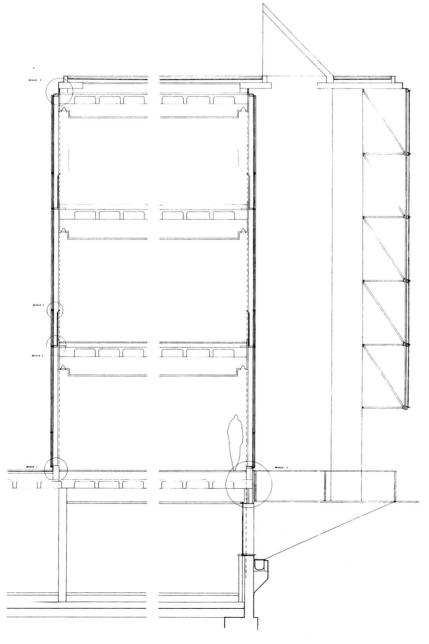

Constructive section of building 1.

Pathé Multiplex Cinema

Koen van Velsen

Pathé Cinema's new cinema center adds to the variety of cultural activities offered in Rotterdam's central Schouwburgplein (Shouwburg Square). The complex contains seven screens with a total seating capacity of 2700. In order to attract a wider clientele than that which normally attends the cinema, a restaurant and a small café have also been included. This transforms the building into a space open to the gen-eral public for longer hours and not just to cinema-goers during showings, as is the case in more traditional cinema centers.

The complex maintains a certain dis-tance psychologically from the square in which it is located. The compact volume never touches the ground. Instead, a wall of glass on the lowest level and on the ele-vation of one part allows for both open space and transparency. The building's

Location: *Rotterdam, Holland.*
Construction dates:
July 1994 - December 1995.
Client: *Pathé Cinemas.*
Collaborators: *Gero Rutten, Marcel Steeghs, Lars Zwant, Okko van der Kam.*
Acoustical engineering: *van Dorsser.*
Project: *A seven-screen cinema center, a restaurant and a café.*
Cross floor surface: *8.473 m².*

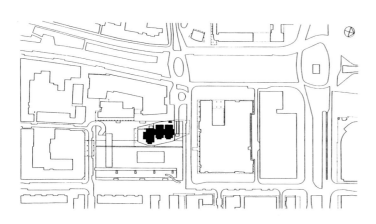

Site plan.

The building's cold industrial
appearance in the daytime contrasts
with its warm appearance at night.

The multiplex cinemas are located
in the Shouwburgplein, a center
of cultural activity in Rotterdam.

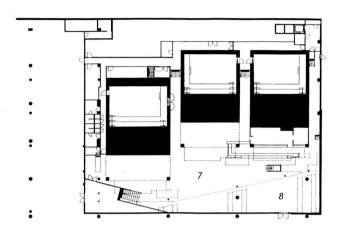

Basement plan.

The free form of the façade wrapping around the central structure creates an interplay of volumes and shapes.

The transparency of the ground level offers a view on the interior.

173

The foyer, touching the
outer façade, is open on
one side to accommodate
connecting staircases.

Close-up of foyer.

Floor plan of access to plaza.

1. Entrance.
2. Box offices.
3. Staircase leading to foyer.
4. Café.
5. Atrium.
6. Restrooms.
7. Grand Café.
8. Access to underground parking.
9. Foyer.

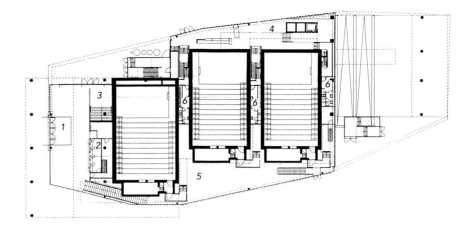

slanting lines give the pedestrian an interesting view of contours leading to the entrance.

Past the box office in the entrance, a set of stairs leads to the large hall on the second floor. This large foyer provides access to all other parts of the building, from the restaurant in the lower level to the cinema halls on the first and second floors and the restrooms. This main space is central to all activities going on in the building, offering spectacular views of the connections between the different levels and the glass perimeter. The foyer offers a great variety of oblique views on the exterior and a play of lines and forms between the glass skin and the upper façade, thus becoming a semi-public extension of the square.

Much of the project has been conditioned by technical factors. The building rests on a preexisting underground parking garage, part of which has been removed to allow space for the restaurant, or Grand Café. It was therefore necessary to leave free space for the parking garage and to make the construction as light as possible. A metallic structure is wrapped in a thin translucent skin, lightening the building both in physical weight and in visual presence. Another technical requirement was soundproofing. Each cinema hall is an isolated box separated from the other halls by corridors and restrooms.

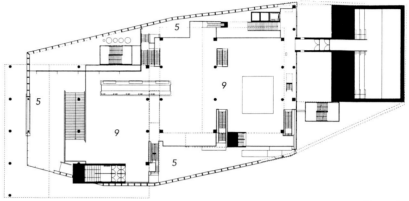

Floor plan - first level.

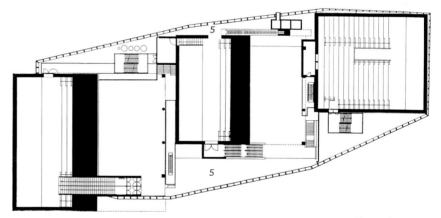

Floor plan - second level.

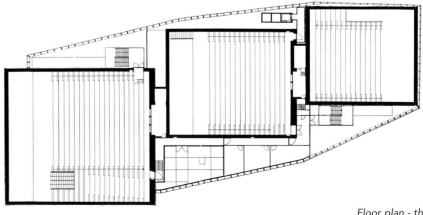

Floor plan - third level.

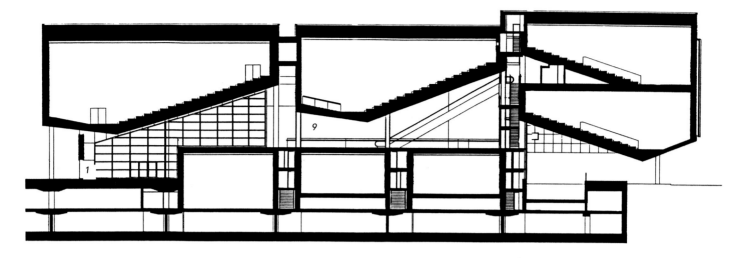

Longitudinal section.

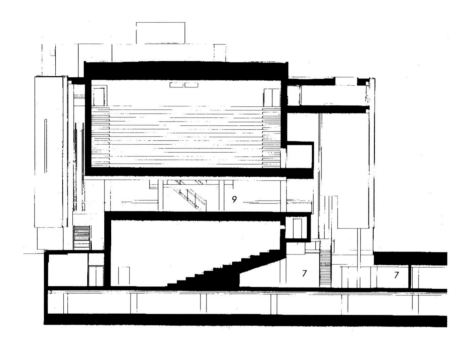

Cross section.

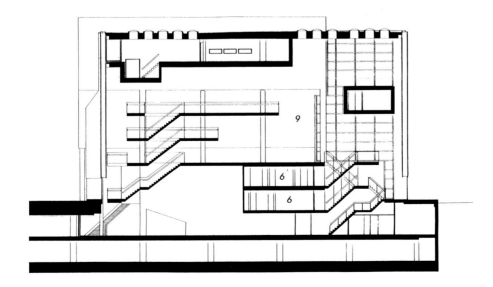

Cross section.

The cinemas are connected to the main structure with rubber blocks to prevent acoustic "leaking."

The façade of undulating polycarbonate cladding has a structure independent from the rest of the building but which wraps around it in free form. The translucent polycarbonate cladding covers both the inside and outside of the surrounding independent wall so that air pipes and fire escapes are partially hidden. The undulating sheets lend the construction an industrial appearance during the day, and at night transform it into a softly-glowing light bulb, becoming the center of attention on the plaza.

The second floor foyer, inundated with light, provides access to all other areas through a spectacular array of staircases.

The space between the cinema halls and the outer wall offers interesting views to the exterior.

View of glowing polycarbonate façade at night.

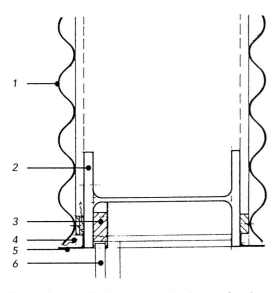

Connecting detail of glass and polycarbonate façade.

1. Semi-transparent polycarbonate cladding.

2. Metal structure.

3. Steel sheet.

4. Ventilation.

5. Steel angle.

6. Layered insulation glass (32 mm).

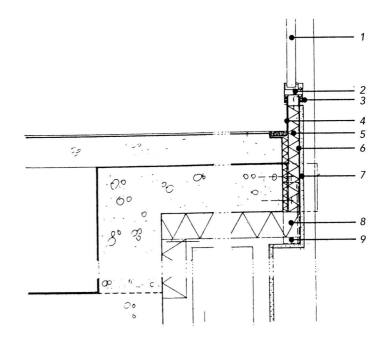

Low edge of glass façade.

1. Layered insulation glass.

2. Steel tube.

3. Propeltone 1313.

4. Stainless steel plating.

5. Polystyrene insulation (50 mm).

6. Humidity proofing.

7. Gypsum board (12.5 mm).

8. Insulation (80 mm).

9. Steel angle.

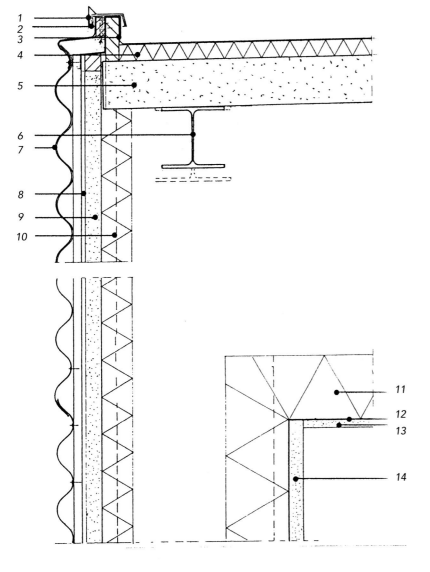

Roof edge at auditorium.

1. Anodized aluminum profile.

2. Ventilation.

3. Roofing.

4. Polystyrene insulation (50 mm).

5. Light-weight concrete (150 mm).

6. Main metal structure.

7. Semi-transparent polycarbonate cladding

8. CEMPANEL (12 mm).

9. Gypsum board (2/3 layers).

10. 100mm mineral wool (100kg/cubic meter).

11. 200mm mineral wool (50kg/cubic meter).

12. Humidity proofing.

13. Gypsum board (2x12.5 mm).

14. Gypsum board (3x12.5 mm).

Nagaoka Lyric Hall

Toyo Ito

On the outskirts of the Japanese city of Nagaoka, on the banks of the river Shinano, in a spot with sweeping vistas of the Echigo mountains, this building takes its place in a wide range of cultural and educational facilities. Although the city already had a large, multi-use hall with seating for 1,500 spectators, the idea here was to create a center, more accessible to the public. In addition to a concert hall for 700 people and a theater with seating for 450, there are also different-sized studios for public use.

Set on a spacious site, the building takes up its position by creating its own personal topography. It takes possession of the site by means of topographical changes, as well as organizing the necessary space for a parking lot to the west. To the south, a small public plaza gives way to a sloping lawn which appears to continue over the roof. Just a narrow, glazed opening imposes itself over the green space. A series of paths follow the topography of the land, leading visitors to an entrance to the upper floor. A tongue of earth cuts into the façade and drops to let light into the first floor foyer.

A longitudinal scheme develops along an east-west axis. The four main volumes

Location: *Nagaoka, Niigata, Japan.*
Date of project: *1993-1994.*
Date of construction: *1994-1997.*
Structures: *KSP- Hanawa Structural Engineers Co, Ltd.*
Brief: *Concert hall (700 persons), theater (450 persons), studios.*
Built surface area: *9,700 square meters.*

Nighttime view.

View from the west.

-theater, concert hall, studios and offices- are laid out on the upper entrance floor, tilted over the line of the façade. This simple corridor scheme leading to the various pieces is embellished as it widens out in contact with each of them. It is a corridor which acts as a foyer, a distributing nucleus, a cafeteria, for the public to enjoy all the complexity of the inner space. This space also expands in section beneath the curved roof of concrete slabs which covers the entire building. Oval-shaped openings draw daylight in at various points, one such being right over the cleft caused by the outside tongue, and another over the space between the two main halls. The latter becomes a small, curving glazed patio which lights the foyer during the day, while at night it is the oval volume of the concert hall which provides the lighting, to become a visible symbol of the building. The hall is clad with translucent polycarbonate panels; when lit up, what initially formed an absolutely blind box not only softens this powerful volume, but also sets itself up as a recognizable sign, an emblem of the building.

The ground floor contains three functional volumes: a block of installations and other services backing onto the site's embankment; a service area for the halls, containing dressing rooms and a private foyer for the artists, with lighting via the oval patio; and lastly an area which communicates with the upper floor, where the various-sized studios are laid out around a naturally lit entrance hall.

Public entrance floor.

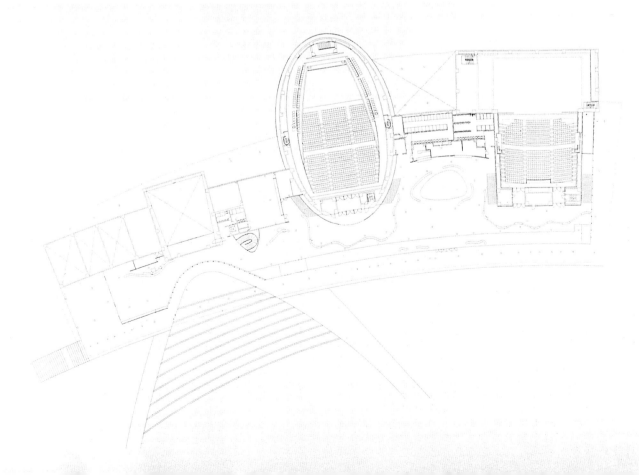

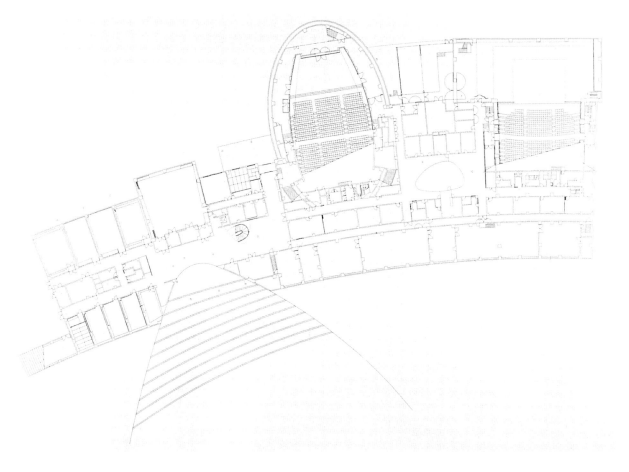

Entrance corridor.

Ground floor.

Views of the patio which lights the foyer.

Following page.

Vestibule.

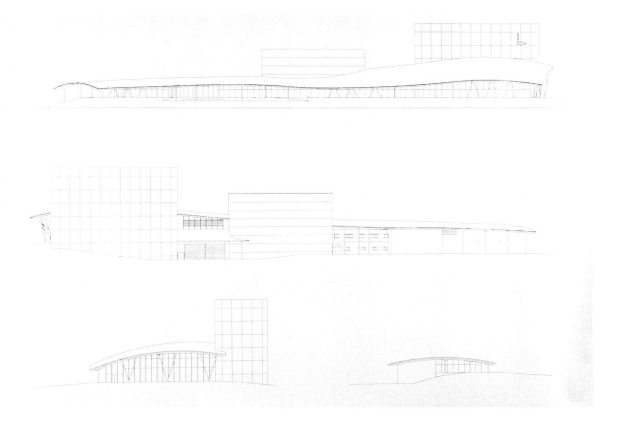

Elevations.

Stairway to the studios.

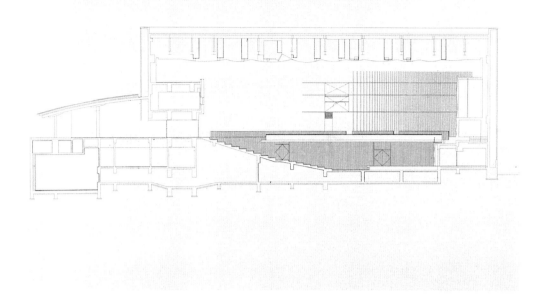

*Cross-section through
the concert hall.*

Concert hall.

Cross-section
through the theater.

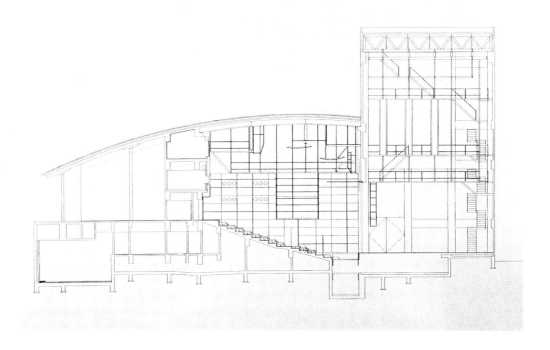

Theater.

Mariano Bayón

1942. Born in Madrid.

1967. Graduated in Architecture from the Escuela Técnica Superior de Arquitectura of Madrid (ETSAM).

1975-1985. Professor of Architectonic Projects at the ETSAM.

1994-1997. Associate Professor at the ETSAM. His work has received numerous prizes and has been exhibited widely.

Ben van Berkel

1957. Born in Utrecht, Holland.

1987. Completes his studies in the Rietveld Academy of Amsterdam and receives a diploma from the Architectural Association of London.

1997. Named Honorary Member of the Bund Deutscher Architecten, BDA.
Has been Visiting Professor at the University of Columbia, New York and at Harvard University. Recently, he has collaborated with the Architectural Association of London.

Arno Brandlhuber

1992. Graduated in Architecture.
Founded his own architectural firm together with B. Kniess of Cologne.

Erik van Egeraat

1956. Born in Amsterdam.

1983. Co-founder of Mecanoo Architects.

1984. Graduated from Delft Technical University.

1995. Founded EEA Erik van Egeraat Associated Architects.

Norman Foster

1935. Born in Manchester, England.

1961. Graduated in Architecture from Manchester University.
Awarded grant to study for Masters Degree in Architecture at Yale University.

1967. Funded Foster Associates.

1968-1983. Collaborated in different projects with Buckminster Fuller.
His work has received numerous prizes throughout the world. He has been Visiting Professor at various universities in the U.S.A and the U.K. Currently, his central office is in London, with subsidiary offices in Glasgow, Berlin, Frankfurt, Hong-Kong and Tokyo.

Von Gerkan, Marg and Partner

1965. Firm founded in Hamburg by Meinhard von Gerkan and Volkwin Marg. The firm has won more than 100 first prizes in the 250 competitions it has entered from 1965 to the present.

Meinhard von Gerkan

1935. Born in Riga.

1956-1964. Studied Architecture in the Universities of Berlin and Braunschweig.

Volkwin Marg

1936. Born in Königsberg

1958-1964. Studied Architecture in the Universities of Berlin and Braunschweig.

Klaus Staratzke

Born in Königsberg.

1963. Graduated in Architecture from the University of Berlin.

1968. Commenced working with von Gerkan and Marg.
Partner in the firm of Von Gerkan, Marg and Partner since 1972.

Itsuko Hasegawa

1964. Graduated in Architecture from the University of Kanto Gakuin, Japan.

1964-1969. Worked in the studio of Kiyonori Kikutake.

1971-1978. Assistant to Kazuo Sinohara at the Tokyo Institute of Technology.

1992-1993. Visiting Professor at the Harvard Graduate School of Design.

Jacques Herzog

1950. Born in Basel, Switzerland.

1975. Graduated in Architecture from the ETH, Zurich.

1977. Assistent to Prof. Dolf Schnebli at the ETH, Zurich.

1978. Begins collaboration with Pierre de Meuron.

1983. Visiting Professor at Cornell University, N.Y.

1989, 1994, 1996-1998. Visiting Professor at the University of Harvard, Cambridge, Mass.

Jean-Marc Ibos, Myrto Vitart

1989. Founded their own firm after spending some years working with Jean Nouvel, where they were involved in projects such as the Tours Congress Centre and the Nemasus residential complex in Nîmes.
After completing the Fine Arts Museum in Lille, their next projects will be a building for Nanterre Fire Department and a Humanities Faculty for the Descartes University of Paris.

Toyo Ito

1941. Born in Japan.

1965. Graduated in Architecture from the University of Tokyo.

1965-1969. Worked with Kiyonori Kikutake Architects and Associates.

1971. Founded his own firm, Urban Robot (URBOT), Tokyo.

1979. Establishes the firm of Toyo Ito and Associates.

Julius Krauss

1989. Graduated in Architecture from the Technical School of Darmstadt.

1989-1993. Worked in various architectural firms in Frankfurt, Düsseldorf, Vienna and Berlin.

1993. Founded his own practise in Darmstadt.

Mecanoo

A group of architects represented by:

Henk Döll, Haarlem, Holland, 1956.

Francine Houben, Sittard, Holland, 1955.

Chris de Weijer, Wageningen, Holland, 1956.

1983-1984. Graduated from the Delft School of Architecture.

Among their projects, the most notable are those dedicated to social housing, such as the neighbourhoods of Kruisplein, Hillekop, Tiendplein and Prinsenland in Rotterdam (1985-1993); also, the recent Economics and Business Faculty in Utrecht.

Pierre de Meuron

1950. Born in Basel, Switzerland.

1975. Graduated in Architecture from the ETH, Zurich.

1977. Assistant to Prof. Dolf Schnebli at the ETH, Zurich.

1978. Begins collaboration with Jacques Herzog.

1989, 1994, 1996-1998. Visiting Professor at the University of Harvard, Cambridge, Mass.

Jean Nouvel

1945. Born at Fumel, France.

1972. Graduated from the École National Supérieur des Beaux-Arts.

1976. Co-founder of the Mars 1976 movement of French architects.

1980. Founder and artistic director of the Paris Biennale d'Architecture.

1987. Awarded the prize for the Best Building of the Year by the Institute of the Arab World.

1995. Honorary Member of RIBA (Royal Institute of British Architects).

Shinichi Ogawa

1955. Born in Yamaguchi, Japan.

1976. Graduated in Architecture from Nihon University.

1977. Graduated in Architecture from Washington State University.

1984-1985. Fellowship Award from Japanese government to study in New York.

1986. Establishes his own firm, in which he has continued to work until the present day.

1994. Assistent Professor at Kinki University.

1995. Honorary Mention in the international competition for the Yokohama Harbour Marine Terminal.

Dominique Perrault

1953. Born in Clermont-Ferrand, France.

1978. Graduated in Architecture from the École Supérieure des Beaux-Arts, Paris.

1979. Certificate in Urban Studies from the École Supérieure des Ponts et Chaussé, Paris.

1980. Masters Degree in History, Ecole des Hautes Etudes en Sciences Sociales, Paris.

1981. Opens office in Paris.

1992. Opens office in Berlin.

1993. Grand Prix National d' Architecture.

Kazuyo Sejima

1956. Born in Ibaraki, Japan.

1981. Graduated in Architecture from the Women's University of Japan.

Begins working with Toyo Ito and Associates.

1987. Founded Kazuyo Sejima and Associates.

Has been Guest Professor at various Japanese Universities.

Rafael Viñoly

Born in Montevideo, Uruguay.

1969. Graduated in Architecture from the Faculty of Architecture and Urban Studies of Buenos Aires, Argentina.

1969. Founded his own firm in Buenos Aires.

1978. Visiting Professor at the University of Washington, and later, at the Univesity of Harvard Graduate School of Design.

1983. Founded Rafael Viñoly Architects, New York.

Günter Zamp Kelp

1967. Graduated in Architecture from Vienna Technical School.

1967. Formed his own architectural firm in Düsseldorf.

Since 1967 has lived and worked in New York (where he was Visiting Professor at Cornell University) and in Berlin (where he is currently Professor in the School of Fine Arts) and in Düsseldorf.